British Letters

Also from Westphalia Press
westphaliapress.org

The Idea of the Digital University

Bulwarks Against Poverty in America

Treasures of London

Avate Garde Politician

L'Enfant and the Freemasons

Baronial Bedrooms

Making Trouble for Muslims

Philippine Masonic Directory ~ 1918

Paddle Your Own Canoe

Opportunity and Horatio Alger

Careers in the Face of Challenge

Bookplates of the Kings

Hymns to the Gods

Freemasonry in Old Buffalo

Original Cables from the Pearl Harbor Attack

Social Satire and the Modern Novel

The Essence of Harvard

The Genius of Freemasonry

A Definitive Commentary on Bookplates

James Martineau and Rebuilding Theology

Bohemian San Francisco

The Wizard

Crime 3.0

Anti-Masonry and the Murder of Morgan

Understanding Art

Spies I Knew

Lodge "Himalayan Brotherhood" No. 459 C.E.

Ancient Masonic Mysteries

Collecting Old Books

Masonic Secret Signs and Passwords

Death Valley in '49

Lariats and Lassos

Mr. Garfield of Ohio

The Wisdom of Thomas Starr King

The French Foreign Legion

War in Syria

Naturism Comes to the United States

New Sources on Women and Freemasonry

Designing, Adapting, Strategizing in Online Education

Gunboat and Gun-runner

Memoirs of a Poor Relation

Espionage!

Bohemian San Francisco

Tales of Old Japan

British Letters

Illustrative of Character and Social Life

Edited by Edward T. Mason

WESTPHALIA PRESS
An imprint of Policy Studies Organization

British Letters: Illustrative of Character and Social Life
All Rights Reserved © 2014 by Policy Studies Organization

Westphalia Press
An imprint of Policy Studies Organization
1527 New Hampshire Ave., NW
Washington, D.C. 20036
info@ipsonet.org

ISBN-13: 978-1-63391-077-5
ISBN-10: 1633910776

Cover design by Taillefer Long at Illuminated Stories:
www.illuminatedstories.com

Daniel Gutierrez-Sandoval, Executive Director
PSO and Westphalia Press

Rahima Schwenkbeck, Director of Marketing and Media
PSO and Westphalia Press

Updated material and comments on this edition
can be found at the Westphalia Press website:
www.westphaliapress.org

BRITISH LETTERS

ILLSTRATIVE OF

CHARACTER AND SOCIAL LIFE

EDITED BY

EDWARD T. MASON

EDITOR OF " HUMOROUS MASTERPIECES," ETC.

★★★

NEW YORK & LONDON

G. P. PUTNAM'S SONS

The Knickerbocker Press

1888

CONTENTS.

THE TOWN.

MISS CATHERINE TALBOT TO MISS ELIZABETH CARTER.

LONDON, April 18, 1747.

. . . There is a sort of enchantment in the air I believe, that makes people avoid each other the moment they are in this vile place, who have been wishing above all things to meet before: for here there is no such thing as friendship, society, or rational conversation. I really am quite out of humor with it. Some of the happiest hours of one's life are those sure which are spent with agreeable conversible friends, in all the ease and freedom of unreserved discourse, not of trifles and visits, actors and drums, but on such subjects as are fit to employ the attention of a reasonable creature, or of such as are at least amusing and engaging. But this sort of society seems to be gone out of the world. In the country we cannot have it, because the people are not there ; and here we cannot have it because everybody is engaged every day in some public place. A woman of excellent sense, and one of the quickest sort, insisted upon it the other night that I should go with her to the play, for the sake of having more of her company than I could possibly enjoy in any other way. . . .

MISS ELIZABETH CARTER TO MISS CATHERINE TALBOT.

LONDON, July 13, 1748.

. . . Pray, dear Miss Talbot, are you all quiet in Oxfordshire? If you are, you can have no idea of the uproar occasioned here by the eclipse, and the strange frights under which people labor. One is stunned all day with the bawling of lamentable prophecies, and a form of prayer. Some run away from London, and others, deeming it the safest place, come to it, and really such as one would imagine should have more sense. The beggars in the streets actually insult folks who refuse to give them small beer, by clapping their hands, and threatening them that the day of judgment will be next Thursday. Others, as I find by a dialogue I overheard in a neighboring court, are of opinion, that all the women in the world, only, are to die. And I lately heard in St. James's place, that a lady, on receiving an invitation to a rout, excused herself, by thinking it really not decent to play cards on that day ; so perhaps she thinks it more decent to put it off till Sunday. . . .

MISS CATHERINE TALBOT TO MISS ELIZABETH CARTER.

LONDON, April 3, 1750.

. . . Young and old, happy and wretched, are all hurrying out of town, on the dreadful, though I trust idle expectation of some fate impending over it to-morrow and Thursday. The gloom that hangs over this town, and will hang over it for some days, induced me to return, that my mother might not be left to encounter it alone, while I was gay and happy, as the most delightful place and society could make me. 'T is surely an idle gloom—the supposition of anybody's being able to fix a day for such awful events, is strangely absurd ; but disbelieve it as much as one will, a more than usual degree of seriousness will sit upon one's mind. There is a poor madman, belonging to Lord Delawar's regiment, who has prophesied a thousand shocking things, and to hear them hawked about this morning almost chilled me ; there was something horrid in it, though the only real horror belonging to it, is the pain it must give to weak, low-spirited people. That I may not sink yours, by a letter written at so critical a juncture, it shall not go till Friday. . . .

April 5th.—The Ides of March are come—but till they are gone too, you shall not have this. Oh the poltroonery of a vile and wicked people ! This poor madman has set about such an alarm, that yesterday the whole town was in hourly expectation of destruction. The churches were full all the morning ; but at night the streets and open places were crowded. Many messages came hither to enquire where my Lord preached, and whether there were not to be prayers in the church at eleven. Thousands spent the night in Hyde Park and Lincoln's Inn Fields. Those who did the least, sat up half the night, except some very few. The moon, stars, and aurora, were well contemplated. But there is something frightful in such a general panic. Once (when the rebels were expected) this spirit of cowardice, had not a gracious providence interposed, must have been very fatal to this town. 'T is grievous to think of the scenes of distress, among good, though weak people, which last night was witness to. All Sunday they were crying about, *The Bishop of London's prayer proper for all Christian families, against the earthquake that is to be on Thursday morn.* The King and Prince have done all they could to check this wildness of fear. I hope it has now spent itself, but if it has, what grief to think that minds so susceptible of strong impressions, should have been thus affected, by such a foolish cause, that they must be ashamed of it, and perhaps of all serious and right impressions along with it. . . .

MISS CATHERINE TALBOT TO MISS ELIZABETH CARTER.

LONDON, December 27, 1754.

I cannot help being so ungenteel as to send you the good wishes of the season, though to any of the fine folks of this town it would certainly be an affront. There was a pretty "World" on this subject last night, accounting with humor, and also with truth, for the general indistinction of all seasons that prevail. I think I could have added a word or two in his own strain. To wish anybody a *merry* Christmas in the old phrase would be quite an absurdity, because that cherry-cheeked, harmless, frank-hearted being, Mirth, has long been banished out of all genteel comanies, to make room for that well-dressed, pale-faced, racketing hag, Diversion, whose smiles are only from the lips outward, and whose joy consists in not being gay but envied. The cherry-cheeked lady, however, I hope, is with you, though divested of all her hoydenish airs. . . .

———

SIR JAMES MACDONALD TO DAVID HUME.

LONDON, April 26, 1765.

The hurry I have been in since my arrival in this place has prevented me from giving myself the pleasure of writing to you. A bare account of my journey must have been the subject of my letter; so that it is at least as well for you that I have not troubled you before, for I believe of all the travels that have been written in any age, mine from Paris to London must have been the dullest, as they were not dignified by any one event of note. Since I have been here I have seen a great many people, and conversed with scarce any; for this is a town where seeing men and living with them are two different things. As I am come here upon business, and have a desire to converse familiarly with several people, the style in which I find everybody live here is to me inexpressibly inconvenient. All the men are formed into clubs ; and as I have not the good fortune to belong to any of them, I have the mortification of knowing where to find all the people I wish to see, without having it in my power to see them. Thus I can only meet by mere accident with any man I want, and cannot possibly live for any time together with any man or any set of men. My business is therefore little advanced ; nor can I guess as yet what aspect my affairs may wear when I have been a month longer here. . . .

MISS ELIZABETH CARTER TO MISS CATHERINE TALBOT.

LONDON, August 9, 1769.

. . . I set out on my city expedition this morning, where I met with an adventure, which, I believe, you will think much more formidable than all the terrors of the Richmond road. I was to call on a person in my way, to accompany me to the South Sea House ; and my nearest route was through Newgate. On going up Snow-Hill I observed a pretty many people assembled, but did not much regard them, till, as I advanced, I found the crowd thicken, and by the time I was got into the midst of them I heard the dreadful toll of St. Sepulchre's bell, and found I was attending an execution. As I do not very well understand the geography of Newgate, I thought if I could push through the postern I should find the coast clear on the other side, but to my utter dismay I found my-self in a still greater mob than before, and very little able to make my way through them. Only think of me in the midst of such heat and suffocation, with the danger of having my arms broke, to say nothing of the company by which I was surrounded, with near 100*l.* in my pocket. In this exigency I applied to one of the crowd for assistance, and while he was hesitating, another man, who saw my difficulty, very good-naturedly said to me: "Come, madam, I will do my best to get you along." To this volunteer in my service, who was tolerably creditable and clean, considering the corps to which he belonged, I most cordially gave my hand ; and without any swearing, or bawling, or bustle whatever, by mere gentle persevering dexterity, he conducted me, I thank God, very safely through. You will imagine that I expressed a sufficient degree of gratitude to my conductor, which I did in the best language I could find; a circumstance which is never thrown away upon the common people, as you will acknowledge from the speech which he made in return: "That all he had done was due to my person, and all he could do was due to my merit." This high strain of complimentary oratory is really no embellishment of my story; but literally what my hero said. What a figure he would have made in the days of chivalry! In the midst of all my perplexities, I could not help remarking a singular circumstance in the discourse of the mob, in speaking of the unhappy criminal, that he was to *die* to-day; and I scarcely once heard the expression of his being to be *hanged.* To trace the cause of this delicacy, is a good problem for the investigators of human nature. . . .

SIR SAMUEL ROMILLY TO JOHN ROGET.

LONDON, June 6, 1780.

. . . The shameful means by which, as I related to you in a former letter, names were procured to the petition for repealing the Catholic Act did not give one any idea that the party could be either very formidable or numerous; but you know how dangerous an engine religion is when employed upon the minds of the ignorant, so dangerous, indeed, that it is formidable in any hands, however weak and contemptible. The Methodists, the followers of Wesley, and the sectaries of Whitfield, were the first, if not to raise, at least to join, the cry against popery; and it should seem, from the effects that have been produced, that no art has been left untried which either could magnify the terrors of the people, by painting to their imagination in the most glaring colors all the horrors of popery, or could infuse among them a mistaken zeal and a dangerous spirit of fanaticism. One way or other, 40,000 persons were prevailed on to sign the petition. Lord George Gordon, that he might give it greater weight, or rather, that he might by violence force it upon the House, advertised in the newspapers as president, and in the name of (what they style themselves) the Protestant Association, the day on which he purposed presenting the petition to the House, at the

same time desiring the attendance of all the
petitioners; and "as no hall is capable of containing 40,000 men" (such were the words of
the advertisement), they were required to assemble in St. George's field, wearing blue cockades as a distinction by which they might know
one another. The concourse of people on the
appointed day, which was last Friday, was as-
tonishing. You know how difficult it is to
judge with accuracy of the numbers of a multitude assembled in an open field. By the
largest computation I have heard, and which is
certainly much exaggerated, there were 100,000
in the fields; but by the most moderate accounts no less than 14,000 accompanied Lord
George to the House of Commons.

When I arrived at Westminster, whither I
went to hear a debate that was to come on in
the House of Lords upon a motion of the Duke
of Richmond, I found the large opening (which
you may remember) between the Parliament
House and Westminster Abbey, all the avenues of the House, and the adjoining streets,
thronged with people wearing blue cockades.
They seemed to consist, in a great measure, of
the lowest rabble; men who, without doubt, not

only had never heard any of the arguments for
or against toleration, but who were utterly ignorant of the purport of the petition. To give
you an instance : A miserable fanatic who ac-
costed me, not indeed with any friendly design,
but to question me where my cockade was,
which I very civilly informed him I had dropped
out of my hat in the crowd, told me that the
reign of the Romans had lasted too long,—the
object of the petition, you know, is only to repeal an Act that passed the year before last.
As I think there is much to be learned by
studying human nature, even in its most humil-
iating and disgusting forms, I would fain have
mingled in a circle which I saw assembled
round a female preacher, who, by her gestures
and actions, seemed to be well persuaded, or
desirous of persuading others, that she was
animated by some supernatural spirit, but I
found it attended with some little danger: the
want of a cockade was a sure indication of a
want of the true faith, and I did not long remain unquestioned as to my religious principles.
My joining, however, in the cry of " No
Popery ! " soon pacified my inquisitors, or rather, indeed, gained me their favor ; for a very

devout butcher insisted upon shaking hands
with me as a token of his friendship. Upon
my getting into the House of Lords, I found
my Lord Mansfield and five or six peers, who
were all that were yet assembled, seemingly in
great consternation from the news they had
just received of Lord Stormont's being in great
danger from the populace. That lord, however, soon made his appearance; he had been
treated rudely, but not very outrageously, by
the mob. Lord Hillsborough and several
other peers came in soon after, with their hair
dishevelled, having lost their bags in the scuffle
they had to get into the House. Lord Bath-
urst, the late Chancellor, was pulled in by
the attendants out of the hands of the populace. Several noblemen, among them Lord
Sandwich, seeing the danger, had returned
home, so that the House was rather thin. The
Duke of Richmond, notwithstanding, rose to
speak upon the motion he was about to make.
He had proceeded in his speech about an hour,
though with frequent interruptions from the
thundering of the mob at the doors of the
House, and the shouting that was heard without, when one of the peers abruptly entered to

inform the Lords that the populace had forced
Lord Boston out of his coach, and that his
life was thought to be in the greatest danger.
Several lords immediately offered to go out and
rescue him, but by the assistance of the attendants and some of the people about the House
this was rendered unnecessary.   Not long after,
word was brought that Lord Ashburnham was
in the same situation, surrounded by the mob
and in great danger; at last, however, he was
dragged into the House over the heads of the
people, and apparently much hurt.   The tumult becoming every moment more violent, it
was found impossible to go on with any business; and at half-past eight the House ad-
journed.   Thus far as to what I was myself a
witness to.

At the House of Commons, the lobby was so
much crowded with the petitioners, that the
members could hardly get in; and none, it is
said, were suffered to pass without giving in
their names to Lord George Gordon, and promising to vote for the repeal.   As soon as the
House sat upon business, the petition was taken
into consideration; but certainly nothing could
be done upon it then, for many members had

been deterred from coming to the House, and
those who were present were far from enjoying
any freedom of debate. A motion was therefore made to defer the further consideration of
it till the following Tuesday, and carried by a
majority of 190 against 9. Lord George then
came into the gallery over the lobby, and ha-
rangued the populace; he told them their
petition was as good as rejected; that if they
expected redress they must keep in a body, or
meet day after day till the Catholic Act was
repealed. Some of his friends, who stood behind him, besought him with the greatest ear-
nestness not to excite the people to measures
which must be destructive to themselves; but
nothing could deter this frantic incendiary, till
he was by violence forced back into the House.
The clamors of the people were now become
so loud, and there appeared among them symptoms of such a dangerous temper, that it was
absolutely necessary to call up the Guards.
This expedient was so far successful that the
lobby and the avenues of the House were soon
cleared; but, without doors, the fury of the
populace was ungovernable. The Bishop of
Lincoln, the Chancellor's brother, was torn out of

his coach as he was going to the House; happily he escaped out of the hands of the mob, and took refuge in a house in Palace Yard; the mob, however, pursued him, broke the windows, and insisted so resolutely on being admitted to search for him, that it was impossible to keep them out any longer than while the Bishop changed his dress, and made his escape over the garden wall. The tumult continued till very late at night, when the mob divided into different parties and broke into three Romish chapels (two of which belonged to ambassadors), tore down the altars, the organs, and decorations of the chapels, brought them out into the street and burned them. Not content with this, at the Sardinian Ambassador's, they carried the fire into the chapel; the inside was presently consumed, but fortunately no other damage was done. . . .

MRS. RICHARD TRENCH TO HER SON.

ELM LODGE, May 29, 1823.

This fine though cold weather finds your mother at Elm Lodge for a week, among blooms and verdure of the highest beauty, with an intention of returning next Saturday to Montague Square. This week would be called a little

oasis in the desert of the town season by some
who consider London as a heartless, dissipated,
hot rendezvous, where so much pleasure is to
be swallowed—no matter with what distaste—
and so many "things to be done," only because
others do them. You and I, however, look on
London with other eyes, as the centre of wholesome, well-regulated liberty, of unfettered intercourse, and of constantly-recurring opportunities and facilities for improvement at all ages.
Would we were there together to enjoy them
as heretofore. Nothing can be purer than the
present predominating pleasures of town, for
all those who are not in the dinner vortex—
seeing fine pictures all the morning, and hearing fine music all the evening. . . .

THOMAS CARLYLE TO ALEXANDER CARLYLE.

PENTONVILLE, December 14, 1824.

. . . Of this enormous Babel of a place I can
give you no account in writing. It is like the
heart of all the universe; and the flood of human
effort rolls out of it and into it with a violence
that almost appals one's very sense. Paris
scarcely occupies a quarter of the ground, and
does not seem to have the twentieth part of the

business. O that our father saw Holborn in a fog!
with the black vapor brooding over it, absolutely
like fluid ink; and coaches and wains and sheep
and oxen and wild people rushing on with bel-
lowings and shrieks and thundering din, as if
the earth in general were gone distracted. To-
day I chanced to pass through Smithfield, when
the market was threefourths over. I mounted
the steps of a door, and looked abroad upon
the area, an irregular space of perhaps thirty
acres in extent, encircled with old dingy brick-
built houses, and intersected with wooden pens
for the cattle. What a scene! Innumerable
herds of fat oxen, tied in long rows, or passing
at a trot to their several shambles; and thousands of graziers, drovers, butchers, cattle-
brokers, with their quilted frocks and long
goads pushing on the hapless beasts; hurrying
to and fro in confused parties, shouting, jost-
ling, cursing, in the midst of rain and *shairn*,
and braying discord such as the imagination
cannot figure. Then there are stately streets
and squares, and calm green recesses to which
nothing of this abomination is permitted to
enter. No wonder Cobbett calls the place a
Wen. It is a monstrous Wen! The thick

smoke of it beclouds a space of thirty square miles; and a million of vehicles, from the dog or cuddy-barrow to the giant-wagon, grind along its streets for ever. I saw a six-horse wain the other day with, I think, Number 200,000 and odds upon it!

There is an excitement in all this which is pleasant as a transitory feeling, but much against my taste as a permanent one. I had much rather visit London from time to time than live in it. There is in fact no *right* life in it that I can find; the people are situated here like plants in a hot-house, to which the quiet influences of sky and earth are never in their unadulterated state admitted. It is the case with all ranks; the carman, with his huge slouch hat hanging half-way down his back, consumes his breakfast of bread and tallow or hog's lard, sometimes as he swags along the streets, always in a hurried and precarious fashion, and supplies the deficit by continual pipes and pots of beer. The fashionable lady rises at three in the afternoon, and begins to live towards midnight. Between these two extremes the same false and tumultuous manner of existence more or less infests all ranks. It seems as if you were forever in "an inn"; the feeling of *home*, in our acceptation of the term, is not known to one of a thousand. You are packed into paltry shells of brick houses (calculated to endure forty years, and then fall); every door that slams to in the street is audible in your most secret chamber; the necessaries of life are hawked about through multitudes of hands, and reach you, frequently adulterated, always at rather more than *twice* their cost elsewhere; people's friends must visit them by rule and measure; and when you issue from your door, you are assailed by vast shoals of quacks, and showmen, and street sweepers, and pick-pockets, and mendicants of every degree and shape, all plying, in noise or silent craft their several vocations, all in their hearts like "lions ravening for their prey." The blackguard population of the place is the most consummately blackguard of any thing I ever saw.

Yet the people are in general a frank, jolly, *well-living*, kindly people. You get a certain way in their good graces with great ease; they want little more with you than now and then a piece of recreating conversation, and you are quickly on terms for giving and receiving it.

Farther, I suspect, their nature or their habits seldom carry or admit them. . . .

THOMAS CARLYLE TO RALPH WALDO EMERSON.

LONDON, April 29, 1836.

. . . I cannot say that this huge blind monster of a city is without some sort of charm for me. It leaves one alone to go his own road unmolested. Deep in your soul you take up your protest against it, defy it, and even despise it, but need not divide yourself from it for that. Worthy individuals are glad to hear your thought, if it have any sincerity ; they do not exasperate themselves or you about it ; they have not even time for such a thing. Nay, in stupidity itself, on a scale of this magnitude, there is an impressiveness, almost a sublimity ; one thinks how, in the words of Schiller, " the very Gods fight against it in vain " ; how it lies on its unfathomable foundation there, inert, yet peptic, nay, eupeptic ; and is a *Fact* in the world, let theory object as it will. Brown-stout, in quantities that would float a seventy-four goes down the throats of men ; and the roaring flood of life pours on ;—over which Philosophy and Theory are but a poor shriek of remonstrance, which oftenest times were wiser, perhaps, to hold its peace. . . .

———

BERNARD BARTON TO MR. CLEMISHA.

LONDON, July 8, 1843.

. . . I never fancy to myself that much, if aught, of *personal* identity can hang about folks in London ; that they can see, hear, smell, or think, talk, and feel, as people do in the country. I can obscurely understand how Cockneys born and bred, or such as are even long resident in Cockaigne, and therefore native to that strange element, may in course of time acquire a sort of borrowed nature, and by virtue of it, a kind of artificial individuality ; but I never was in London long enough to get at this, and have always seemed, when there, *not to be myself*, but very much as if I were walking in a dream, or like a bit of sea-weed blown off some cliff or beach, and drifting with the current—one knew not why or how. In a coffee-room, up one of those queer long dark inn yards, I have felt more like myself ;—there is more of quiet ; folks often sit in boxes apart, and talk in a kind of undertone ; or when they do not, the united effect of so many voices becomes a sort of in-

distinct hum or buzz, relieved at intervals by
the swinging to and fro of the coffee-room door,
the clatter of plates, the jingle of glasses, or the
rustle of the newspaper often turned over. I
have spent an hour or two after my fashion in
this way, at the Four Swans, Belle Sauvage,
Bolt in Ton, Spread Eagle, and other coach-
houses, by no means unpleasantly, seemingly
reading the paper, and sipping my tea or coffee,
wine or toddy, but really catching some amusing scraps of the talk going on around, and
speculating on the characters of the talkers.
But the greatest luxury London had to give, is
gone with my poor old friend Allan Cunning-
ham. It was worth something to steal out of
the din and hubbub of crowded streets into
those large, still, cathedral-like rooms of Chan-
trey's, populous with phantom-like statues, or
groups of statues, as large or larger than life ;
some tinted with dust and time, others of
spectral whiteness, but all silent and solemn ;
to roam about among these, hearing nothing
but the distant murmur of rolling carriages,
now and then the clink of the workman's chisel
in some of the yards or workshops, but chiefly
the low, deliberate, often amusing, and always

interesting talk of honest Allan, in broad Scotch. A morning of this sort, was well worth going up to London on purpose for.

———

MRS. THOMAS CARLYLE TO MRS. RUSSELL.

CHELSEA, July 15, 1850.

. . . There has been a dreadful racket here this season—worse, I think, than in any London season I ever lived through—it has seemed to me sometimes as if the town must burst into spontaneous combustion. All the people of my acquaintance who come to London occasionally, have come this year at one time, spoiling the pleasure I should have had in seeing them individually by presenting themselves all in a rush—in fact, our house, for two months back, has been like an inn, only "no money taken," and I feel like a landlady after an election week. And the balls and parties all round one, to certain of which I had to go, for the sake of what is called "keeping up one's acquaintance," have been enough to churn one into a sort of human "trifle." Peel's death came like a black cloud over this scene of so-called "gaieties," for a few days, but only for a few days. Nothing leaves a long impression here. People dare not let themselves think or feel in this centre of frivolity and folly ; they would go mad if they did, and universally commit suicide ; for to " take a thocht and mend " is far from their intention. . . .

SYDNEY SMITH TO MISS GEORGINA HARCOURT.

LONDON, 1838.

. . . The summer and the country, dear Georgina, have no charms for me. I look forward anxiously to the return of bad weather, coal fires, and good society in a crowded city. I have no relish for the country ; it is a kind of healthy grave. I am afraid you are not exempt from the delusions of flowers, green turf, and birds ; they all afford slight gratification, but not worth an hour of rational conversation ; and rational conversation in sufficient quantities is only to be had from the congregation of a million of people in one spot. . . .

CHARLES LAMB TO THOMAS MANNING.

LONDON, November 28, 1800.

I have received a very kind invitation from Lloyd and Sophie to go and spend a month with them at the Lakes. Now it fortunately happens (which is so seldom the case) that I have spare cash by me, enough to answer the expenses of so long a journey; and I am determined to get away from the office by some means. . . .

For my part, with reference to my friends northward, I must confess that I am not romance-bit about *Nature*. The earth, and sea, and sky (when all is said) is but as a house to dwell in. If the inmates be courteous, and good liquors flow like the conduits at an old coronation, if they can talk sensibly and feel properly, I have no need to stand staring upon the gilded looking-glass (that strained my friend's purse-strings in the purchase), nor his five-shilling print over the mantlepiece of old Nabbs the carrier (which only betrays his false taste). Just as important to me (in a sense) is all the furniture of my world—eye-pampering, but satisfies no heart. Streets, streets, streets, markets, theatres, churches, Covent Gardens, shops sparkling with pretty faces of industrious milliners, neat sempstresses, ladies cheapening, gentlemen behind counters lying, authors in the street with spectacles, George Dyers (you may know them by their gait), lamps lit at night, pastry-cooks' and silver-smiths' shops, beautiful Quakers of Pentonville, noise of coaches, drowsy cry of mechanic watchman at night, with bucks reeling home drunk ; if you happen to wake at midnight, cries of Fire and Stop thief ; inns of court, with their learned air, and halls, and butteries, just like Cambridge colleges ; old book-stalls, Jeremy Taylors, Burtons on Melancholy, and Religio Medicis on every stall. These are thy pleasures, O London with-the-many-sins! . . . .

CHARLES LAMB TO WILLIAM WORDSWORTH.

LONDON, January 30, 1801.

I ought before this to have replied to your very kind invitation into Cumberland. With you and your sister I could gang anywhere ; but I am afraid whether I shall ever be able to afford so desperate a journey. Separate from the pleasure of your company, I don't much care if I never see a mountain in my life. I have passed all my days in London, until I have formed as many and intense local attachments, as any of you mountaineers can have done with dead nature. The lighted shops of the Strand and Fleet Street ; the innumerable trades, tradesmen, and customers, coaches,

wagons, playhouses ; all the bustle and wicked-
ness round Covent Garden ; the watchmen,
drunken scenes, rattles ; life awake, if you are
awake, at all hours of the night ; the impossi-
bility of being dull in Fleet Street ; the crowds,
the very dirt and mud, the sun shining upon
houses and pavements ; the print-shops, the old
book-stalls, parsons cheapening books, coffee-
houses, steams of soups from kitchens, the
pantomimes—London itself a pantomime and
a masquerade—all these things work themselves into my mind, and feed me without a
power of satiating me. The wonder of these
sights impels me into night-walks about her
crowded streets, and I often shed tears in the
motley Strand from fulness of joy at so much
life. All these emotions must be strange to
you ; so are your rural emotions to me. But
consider, what must I have been doing all my
life, not to have lent great portions of my heart
with usury to such scenes ?

My attachments are all local, purely local—I
have no passion (or have had none since I was
in love, and then it was the spurious engender-
ing of poetry and books) to groves and valleys.
The rooms where I was born, the furniture

which has been before my eyes all my life, a
book-case which has followed me about like a
faithful dog (only exceeding him in knowledge)
wherever I have moved—old chairs, old tables,
streets, squares, where I have sunned myself;
my old school,—these are my mistresses—have
I not enough, without your mountains? I do
not envy you. I should pity you, did I not
know that the mind will make friends with any
thing. Your sun, and moon, and skies, and
hills, and lakes, affect me no more, or scarcely
come to me in more venerable characters than
as a gilded room with tapestry and tapers,
where I might live with handsome visible objects. I consider the clouds above me but as a
roof beautifully painted, but unable to satisfy
the mind ; and, at last, like the pictures of the
apartment of a connoisseur, unable to afford
him any longer a pleasure. So fading upon
me, from disuse, have been the beauties of
Nature, as they have been confinedly called ;
so ever fresh and green and warm are all the
inventions of men, and assemblies of men in
this great city. . . .

THE COUNTRY.

MISS MARY LAMB TO MRS. MARY COWDEN CLARKE.

NEWINGTON, 1820.

. . . It is so many years since I have been out of town in the spring, that I scarcely knew of the existence of such a season. I see every day some new flower peeping out of the ground, and watch its growth ; so that I have a sort of intimate friendship with each. I know the effect of every change of weather upon them,—have learned all their names, the duration of their lives, and the whole progress of their domestic economy. My landlady, a nice, active old soul that wants but one year of eighty,—and her daughter, a rather aged young gentlewoman,—are the only laborers in a pretty large garden ; for it is a double house, and two long strips of ground are laid into one, well stored with fruit trees, which will be in full blossom the week after I am gone, and flowers as many as can be crammed in, of all sorts and

kinds. But flowers are flowers still; and I
must confess I would rather live in Russell
Street all my life, and never set my foot but
on the London pavement, than to be doomed
always to enjoy the silent pleasures I now do.
We go to bed at ten o'clock—late hours are
life-shortening things; but I would rather run
all risks, and sit every night—at some places I
could name—wishing in vain at eleven o'clock
for the entrance of the supper tray, than
be always up and alive at eight o'clock breakfast, as I am here. We have a scheme to rec-
oncile these things. We have an offer of a very
low-rented lodging a mile nearer town than
this. Our notion is, to divide our time in al-
ternate weeks between quiet rest and dear
London weariness. We give an answer to-
morrow; but what that will be, at this present
writing I am unable to say. In the present
state of our undecided opinion, a very heavy
rain that is now falling may turn the scale.
" Dear rain, do go away," and let us have a fine,
cheerful sunset to argue the matter fairly in.
My brother walked seventeen miles yesterday,
before dinner; and notwithstanding his long
walk to and from the office, we walk every

evening; but I by no means perform in this way so well as I used to do. A twelve-mile walk, one hot Sunday morning, made my feet blister; and they are hardly well now. . . .

CHARLES LAMB TO THOMAS MANNING.

LONDON, September 24, 1802.

Since the date of my last letter, I have been a traveller. A strong desire seized me of visiting remote regions. My first impulse was to go and see Paris. It was a trivial objection to my aspiring mind, that I did not understand a word of the language, since I certainly intend some time in my life to see Paris, and equally certainly never intend to learn the language; therefore that could be no objection. . . . And my final resolve was a tour to the Lakes. I set out with Mary to Keswick, without giving Coleridge any notice; for my time being precious did not admit of it. He received us with all the hospitality in the world, and gave up his time to show us all the wonders of the country. He dwells upon a small hill by the side of Keswick, in a comfortable house, quite enveloped on all sides by a net of mountains; great floundering bears and monsters they

seemed, all couchant and asleep. We got in
in the evening, travelling in a post-chaise from
Penrith in the midst of a gorgeous sunshine,
which transmuted all the mountains into colors
purple, etc., etc. We thought we had got into
fairy-land. But that went off (as it never came
again—while we stayed we had no more fine
sunsets) ; and we entered Coleridge's comfortable study just in the dusk, when the mountains
were all dark with clouds upon their heads.
Such an impression I never received from objects of sight before, nor do I suppose that I
can ever again. Glorious creatures, fine old
fellows, Skiddaw, etc. I never shall forget ye,
how ye lay about that night, like an intrench-
ment ; gone to bed, as it seemed for the night,
but promising that ye were to be seen in the
morning. Coleridge had got a blazing fire
in his study, which is a large, antique, ill-shaped
room, with an old-fashioned organ, never played
upon, big enough for a church, shelves of scattered folios, an Æolian harp, and an old sofa,
half-bed, etc. And all looking out upon the
last fading view of Skiddaw and his broad-
breasted brethren : what a night ! Here we
stayed three full weeks. . . .

Vol. III.

We have clambered up to the top of Skiddaw, and I have waded up the bed of Lodore.
In fine I have satisfied myself that there is
such a thing as that which tourists call *romantic*, which I very much suspected before ; they
make such a spluttering about it, and toss their
splendid epithets around them, till they give
as dim a light as at four o'clock next morning
the lamps do after an illumination. Mary was
excessively tired when she got about half-way
up Skiddaw, but we came to a cold rill (than
which nothing can be imagined more cold, running over cold stones), and with the reinforce-
ment of a draught of cold water she surmounted
it most manfully. Oh, its fine black head, and
the bleak air atop of it, with a prospect of
mountains all about and about, making you
giddy ; and then Scotland afar off, and the
border countries so famous in song and ballad !
It was a day that will stand out like a mountain, I am sure, in my life. But I am returned
(I have now been come home near three weeks
—I was a month out), and you cannot conceive
the degradation I felt at first from being accustomed to wander free as air among mountains,
and bathe in rivers without being controlled by

any one, to come home and *work*. I felt very
little. I had been dreaming I was a very great
man. But that is going off, and I find I shall
conform in time to that state of life to which
it has pleased God to call me. Besides, after
all, Fleet Street and the Strand are better
places to live in for good and all than amidst
Skiddaw. Still, I turn back to those great
places where I wandered about, participating
in their greatness. After all I could not *live*
in Skiddaw. I could spend a year—two, three
years among them, but I must have a prospect
of seeing Fleet Street at the end of that time,
or I should mope and pine away, I know. Still,
Skiddaw is a fine creature. . . .

CHARLES LAMB TO SAMUEL TAYLOR COLERIDGE.

LONDON, September 8, 1802.

. . . We got home very pleasantly on Sunday. Mary is a good deal fatigued, and finds
the difference of going to a place and coming
from it. I feel that I shall remember your
mountains to the last day I live. They haunt
me perpetually. I am like a man who has been
falling in love unknown to himself, which he
finds out when he leaves the lady. I do not

remember any very strong impression while
they were present; but, being gone, their me-
mentos are shelved in my brain. . . .

———

CHARLES LAMB TO WILLIAM WORDSWORTH.

ENFIELD, January 22, 1830.

. . . Oh! never let the lying poets be believed
who 'tice men from their cheerful haunts of
streets, or think they mean it not of a country
village. In the ruins of Palmyra I could gird myself up to solitude, or muse to the snorings of
the Seven Sleepers; but to have a little teasing
image of a town about one: country folks that
do not look like country folks: shops two
yards square, half a dozen apples, and two
penn'orth of overlooked ginger-bread, for the
lofty fruiterers of Oxford Street; and for the
immortal book and print stalls a circulating
library that stands still, where the show-picture
is a last year's valentine, and whither the fame
of the last ten Scotch novels has not yet trav-
elled—(marry, they just begin to be conscious
of the "Redgauntlet")—to have a new plas-
tered flat church, and to be wishing that it was
but a cathedral! The very blackguards here
are degenerate, the topping gentry stock-

brokers; the passengers too many to insure
your quiet, or let you go about whistling or
gaping; too few to be the fine, indifferent pa-
geants of Fleet Street. Confining, room-keep-
ing, thickest winter is yet more bearable here
than the gaudy months. Among one's books
at one's fire by candle, one is soothed into
an oblivion that one is not in the country ; but
with the light the green fields return, till I gaze,
and in a calenture can plunge myself into St.
Giles'. Oh ! let no native Londoner imagine
that health and rest, and innocent occupation,
interchange of converse sweet and recreative
study, can make the country any thing better
than altogether odious and detestable. A garden was the primitive prison, till man with
Promethean felicity and boldness luckily sinned
himself out of it. Thence followed Babylon,
Nineveh, Venice, London ; haberdashers, gold-
smiths, taverns, playhouses, satires, epigrams,
puns,—these all came in on the town part and
the thither side of innocence. . . .

MRS. SARA COLERIDGE TO AUBREY DE VERE.

WOLVERHAMPTON, July 9, 1850.

When we had passed Birmingham and entered the region of cinders and groves of chim-

neys, I thought it almost equalled the hideous-
ness of a certain manufacturing portion of
Lancashire. On the side of Tentenhall and
Penn, Staffordshire has its share of sylvan
beauty. The Worcestershire hills rise in several ranges faintly blue on the horizon. This
house is all built (by Rickman) and furnished
in the olden style, with great elegance and
harmony of effect; the painted glass and old
carved oak furniture are fine in their way, and
the prospect from the windows reminds one of
pictures of the garden of Boccaccio: the vistas
are well managed, so as to *seem* ended only by
the Wrekin in the distance; the turf is in high
perfection,—such an expanse of emerald velvet
I scarce ever saw before; and the cedars scattered among the other trees delight me especially. I have been so long shut out from
scenes of this kind that the place appears to
me a finer one perhaps than it does to those
who go from one smooth, ornate country-seat
to another, year by year. I do feel, however,
the want of water. In the Dingle, a picturesque glen in the grounds of Mr. C——, of
Badger, water has its due part in the scene,
now in the foamy water-fall, now in the wide,

quiet, gleamy pool, that reflects the sky and
the branching of the tall, picturesque trees
around. Yesterday we visited Boscobel, and
E—— crept down into the hole where Charles
II. is *said* to have hidden himself. I tried to
go, too, but felt too much stifled to proceed.
I was pleased to see, in returning by the artificial lake at Chillington, which made me think
of Curragh Chase and a certain poem of yours,
that Mr. G——, the owner, allows the people
of the neighborhood to disport themselves
there on a certain day every week. How much
more lively enjoyment he must have in seeing
a crowd of people whom his bounty has refreshed, than in keeping the whole spacious
domain to himself all the week round, closed
up in silent, melancholy state, no one going
near that fine sheet of water embosomed in
woods from hour to hour. Surely men will, in
the course of time, become wiser about such
matters than they have been, and frame for
themselves deeper and keener pleasures, more
stirring and expansive enjoyments, than wealth
and large possessions have brought to our
grandees for the most part. There is something to my feelings always deeply sad and

sombre in the sight of a large domain belonging to some stately reserved proprietor, living
alone there with but few domestic servants.   It
puts me in mind of the poor, bounded nature
of our existence here, when it is regarded in a
worldly point of view.   There is great amusement in constructing a fine house and superin-
tending the laying-out of a large pleasure
ground, such as my friend Mr. M—— has had
here ; but when all is done, and the place perfect in its way, I fancy the lawns and groves
breathing sadness to the spirit of a proprietor,
which is never felt when we gaze upon the
wild woods and fields with a sense that we are
not bound to enjoy them because they are
ours. . . .

CHARLES JAMES MATHEWS TO HIS MOTHER.

GLENFISHIE,* September 25, 1833.

. . . A day or two after our return from
the trip to Loch A'an, . . . preparations
were made for flitting from the Doune, to take
up our residence in a romantic glen about fifteen
miles off, where the Duchess loves to dwell and
lay out her pin money.   Orders were given that

* Mathews was the guest of the Duke and Duchess of Bed-
ford, at their Highland home.

all *grande toilette* should be suspended until further notice, and that those who were not prepared to rough it should remain behind. Leaving the ladies to get there their own way, we gentlemen at break of day (that is between eight and nine) set off on our shaggy ponies with the intention of shooting our way over the mountain tops to the glen. The day was beautiful, and the road every thing that could be desired. Perhaps I ought here to explain that whenever I mention roads I mean those which we make ourselves, for even a sheep path is almost a rarity over these wild mountains. After a most fatiguing ascent, we reached the ptarmigan hills, where the party dispersed in various directions in quest of game. Having ascertained the direction of the glen I left them and proceeded alone across the mountains, with the day before me to enjoy the magnificent views which presented themselves on all sides. After a most delightful walk I entered the narrow pass leading to the glen, through the centre of which foamed and tumbled the River Fishie, forming in its course an endless variety of waterfalls. Towards evening, having waded four or five times up to my middle through the stream, an amusement of such frequent occurrence here as hardly to be worth mentioning, I entered that part of the pass which is called *par excellence* "the" glen. There I found the ladies. The Duchess, Lady Rachel, and the maids had arrived a little before me in their tilt-cart; Miss Balfour and Lady Georgiana having, under the escort of a guide, walked all the way from the Doune. I was immediately conducted to view the habitation, and certainly never saw any thing half so original in conception or so perfect in execution as the whole thing. The appearance was that of a small Indian settlement, consisting of one low building containing three or four bedrooms and the kitchen, etc., and two smaller ones of one room each, the one being dining-room, parlor, drawing-room, and hall, and the others containing two beds for ladies. The rest of the settlement was composed of tents, various in size and in use. The buildings themselves looked like the poorest peasants' cottages. The walls made of turf and overgrown with foxglove, and the roof of untrimmed spars of birch. The apartments within corresponded perfectly with their exterior. Every thing of rough unpeeled birch, except the uncovered turf walls. The fires of peat and clear-burning fir blazed away upon the ground, in short, every thing bespeaking the habitation of some tasteful wood-cutter. The drawing-room was of tolerable length and height, but the bedrooms only just large enough to turn round in. The beds of the ladies resembled small presses or chests of drawers, with mattresses stuffed with heather and pillows of the same let into them like the hammocks of a vessel. The gentlemen's apartments were in tents, each containing two small heather couches, side by side on tressels, one small table and a wash-hand-stand and foot-bath, but no chairs, curtains, nor looking-glass. The carpet was of turf, upon which our wardrobes were arranged, protected by occasional pieces of wood in case of promiscuous or superfluous damp. Can you conceive all this, or do you think me inventing? Here we have been now above a week living on venison, grouse, hares, partridges, black-cock, ptarmigan, plovers, salmon, char, pike, trout, beef, mutton, pork, etc., etc., all killed by ourselves and nearly on the spot; at any rate all (even red deer and ptarmigan) within a mile of the house. The

ladies have only the dress of the country shape
and material.   Bedgown of some light material,
generally striped; a blue cloth or gray stuff
petticoat, very short; scarlet, gray, and blue
stockings, aprons and mittens, and snoods of
red or blue through their hair, and colored
handkerchiefs protect their heads from rain and
wind; but bonnets and caps are unknown.
The gentlemen wear the kilts, and, in short,
every thing is picturesque in the extreme.   It is
without any exception the most delightful sort
of life I have ever seen or experienced.   Amusements of every sort are constantly going on.
The guitar is in great request, and a small piano
of two octaves, made on purpose for travelling,
is constantly going.   Lord Ossulston and Miss
Balfour both sing beautifully, and we get up
songs, duets, and trios without end.   A more
charming spot for midnight serenading cannot
be imagined. . . .

On the other side of the Fishie, about a
quarter of a mile from us, is another, but far
inferior dwelling, formerly occupied by the
Duchess, and built by her, but now the residence of Captain Ross, with whom is Mr. Ellis
and his son.   You remember Ellis well, and I

think with unfavorable impression, but I can assure you that we much wronged him, for he is a most kind, good-natured, agreeable person. He and his son have taken the shooting ground which joins that of Rothiemurchus in conjunction with Ross, and are capital neighbors. Our party went over on Monday to dine with them. One of our tents was sent across to form the banqueting hall, and each man took his knife and fork with him. The day turned out tremendous. Torrents of rain and tempests of wind succeeded each other, till we began to fear that the river would be too much swollen to allow us to attempt the fords, three of which were to be passed. At seven o'clock, however, in the midst of a hurricane, we set off. The tilt-car held six, and the rest were accommodated on ponies. The passing through the rocky bed of the river would, I think, have suited you perfectly. The cart, not particularly easy in itself, falling from stone to stone, and threatening an upset any moment; the water tearing down with the greatest rapidity, and filling the bottom of the cart; and the wind, with the most frightful gusts, positively rocking it to and fro. On the other side we were met by the piper, who walked before us to the house, and half a dozen gillies walked in procession on each side of the cart, the horsemen following. On reaching the Wooden House, as it is called, anticipating rather uneasy quarters in the tent, we were most agreeably surprised by finding that the idea had been abandoned, and that Ellis's bedroom had been cleared out, beds removed, and guns unshipped, to form a dining-room. A tremendous fire of wood and peat blazed upon the hearth, and a long, well-secured table stood in the middle of the room, well covered with candles of wax stuck in turnip candlesticks of the most elegant workmanship; on the timbers of the roof other similar candlesticks were fixed, so that the illumination was splendid. The banquet was profuse and the dressing exquisite. Venison in every shape and disguise; wild game and fish of every sort and description; ending with cranberry and blaeberry tarts, and all sorts of clotted cream, custards, apple-puddings, and turnip-pies. Lots of champagne, claret, moselle, ices, etc., were disposed of, not to allude to the bottled porter, ale, soda-water, and all those sort of luxuries, which abounded. The feast was exceedingly gay, the piper playing all the time outside, and an enormous bonfire of birch and fir-trees kept constantly alive, in spite of the most tremendous unceasing hurricane which raged without. After the ladies retired, mulled claret and whiskey toddy were introduced ; and coffee and tea, with songs and choruses, welcomed their return. All these things having been duly honored, gillies were despatched to see in what state the river was, as it was strongly suspected that it might have increased so as to prevent our return. The report, however, justified an attempt—though not a thing to be done without great hazard, in consequence of the darkness of the night, the rapidity of the torrent, and the hurricane which raged—and preparations were made for the undertaking. The tilt-cart was brought out, and the ladies and boys were packed within it; the gentlemen mounted their ponies, and our hosts ordered out their horses to escort the party. The rain descended in torrents, notwithstanding which the bonfire still burnt brightly, and it illuminated an immense space around it, with the drenched Highlanders plainly discernible in the midst of the glare. All being in order, the cavalcade set out, preceded by a dozen gillies bearing immense blazing fire-brands of fir branches, next the pipes, playing lustily before the tilt-cart, which rocked about through the mud and moss most alarmingly, followed by the horsemen and a second detachment of blazing branches. The effect was very fine indeed; and the commanding figure of Ross—a sort of O. Smith man—in his Scotch bonnet, large smuggler's jacket, and bare legs and tartan hose, mounted on a large black charger, who rode about twenty yards in front of the whole party, completed the procession. In spite of all difficulties we reached our own quarters in safety, and within our tents that night many were the glasses of whiskey toddy, and pipes, and cigars which were consumed by the survivors. . . .

What do you think of ladies of fashion going through, for their pleasure and amusement, such real hardships as I have described to you? I think it the most surprising thing I ever met with. Nothing daunts them, and no fatigue is too much for them.

The night after the dinner party we gave a ball, and all the lads and lasses in the neighborhood (that is about a dozen in all, being the population of ten or twelve miles round) were invited. Two fiddlers and a piper worked away from eight in the evening till six in the morning, when the delicate young ladies, who had walked ten miles to the ball in the rain, and waded through three fords in their way, set out again, after dancing all night, to walk back—through the three fords—ten miles to their work. There are many people would call this making a labor of a pleasure, but they find pleasure in the labor. The quantity of whiskey toddy drank upon the occasion you may suppose was not small, but there was no one, I understand, *very* fou. The Duchess, notwithstanding a slight failing,—from a previous accident—in her knee, danced as well as any one of the party, and in the reels decidedly beat all. The young ladies are sylphs. As to myself, I must own I am amazed. The manner in which I walk over the hills, ford the rivers, scale the rocks, and dance reels is past belief. I feel just as strong, and able to support fatigue, as I ever was in my life, and the more I take the stronger I am. . . .

Vol. III.

MRS. SARA COLERIDGE TO AUBREY DE VERE.

MARGATE, June 20, 1851.

. . . My general health has derived as much benefit from my stay here as it usually does from a seaside visit. I walk an hour in the morning, and in the evening an hour or fifty minutes. I could do more than this in the way of exercise, but, though my strength would allow of it, I fear that it might not be prudent.

The weather was quite wintry—a spring temperature, with the squally look and sound of winter—during the first nine or ten days of our stay. Now it begins to be Junish : the butterflies are abroad, especially the azure ones, that seem to be animated bits cut out of the sapphire of the still, blue sea; the corn-poppy rears its head, that was hung down like that of an Eastern slave making a low obeisance, and discloses its scarlet head-gear; while the blossomed beans look up and seem to *stare* at us with their clear black eye, the jetty iris surrounded by a snowy cornea. Have you ever observed this in the bean-blossom ? it is really pretty to behold. The sweet odors from the bean-fields, and from little gardens full of stocks, carnations, roses, gilly-flowers, pinks, and southernwood, which

we pass on our cliff walk, are an agreeable contrast to the vile ones which annoy us when we
enter the town to post letters or to get a book
from one of the libraries. . . .

FRANCIS HORNER TO HIS SISTER.

CRICKHOWEL, August 21, 1807.

The last account I gave of myself was from
Clifton ; since that, Murray and I have come
by way of Chepstow and Abergavenny to this
pretty village of Crickhowel, which is just
within Wales, upon the borders of Brecknock-
shire. We do not mean to go any farther, but
have taken lodgings for four or five days, till
we turn eastward again to London.

The situation of this village is at the head of
a pass leading from Abergavenny into the
mountainous country, and five or six beautiful
valleys, stretching into that country in various
directions, end and meet here. They are more
green than any thing that is to be seen to the
east of Somersetshire ; and the uplands are enclosed and cultivated almost to the top of the
hills. The sides are covered with little farm-
houses and their orchards, and very small
patches of wheat ; and every field almost has a
footpath. I am very apt to think the last beau-

tiful country I have seen the most beautiful I
ever saw; so that you cannot rely very much
upon my choice; that, however, is my present
way of thinking.   We wanted a place to be
quiet for a short time, and we seem to have
pitched upon this one, fortunately.   Our plan
is this: we go out to walk about one o'clock in
the day, spending a long morning (for we get
up rather early) in a long breakfast, and getting
through some business about the plans for re-
forming the Court of Session; we return to
dinner before it becomes dark, usually about an
hour and a half after the time we ordered, lest
we should acquire any rural habits of punctu-
ality; and, after dining as well as we can in all
respects, contrive to get another walk before
going to bed.   We dine at a little inn, where
there is a ball-room, however, as there is everywhere in this part of the world; our lodgings
are with an old dapper gentleman, the tax-gatherer (I believe)—quite a character, addicted from
his youth upwards to angling and music. . . .

MRS. MARIA HARE TO AUGUSTUS J. C. HARE.
LIME, May 1, 1844.

Do you remember the garlands you liked so
much to see on May Day? This year I thought

the children would have more enjoyment in
dancing round a May-pole. So one was put up
in front of Mrs. Piper's school, crowned with
flowers, with a blue flag at the top and a great
bunch of gorse. Inside the schoolroom the
beams and walls were hung with evergreens,
and from these were suspended many beautiful
garlands of flowers. At the end of the room
was a sort of bower, with a doll dressed as
Queen of the May, and on the tables and desk,
jars filled with flowers, and moss and nosegays
tied up in bunches. At three o'clock all the
children of Mrs. Piper's and Mrs. Coleman's
school, sixty-eight in number, sate down on the
benches, and had tea and bread-and-butter and
large buns—Lea, Anne, and Susan waiting on
them. The children had wished to crown Mrs.
Piper as Queen of the May, but she took the
garland and put it on Emily Elphick, and
wanted her to wear it forever. But the poor
little girl was so distressed in the thought that
she had any honor above the other girls, and
the fact that they might be pained by it, that
she cried bitterly, and would not be satisfied
till she had made a crown for each of her own
class as pretty as her own. When the tea was

over, they sang a May-song which I had made
for them.   Then they all went into the little
court, and danced round the May-pole, and
played at their games, and were, I think, very
happy.

It could not have been a more beautiful May
Day.   The nightingales are singing so joyously
in the copse, and it is covered now with blue-
bells and orchises.   Your garden has a beautiful periwinkle in it, and the great horse-chestnut
is full of flowers, and like the middle of summer
with its leaves.

SIR SAMUEL ROMILLY TO MADAME D——

ABERGAVENNY, April 18, 1789.

I write to you, Madam, from a place, the
name of which is, I fancy, hardly known to
you.   It is a little town on the borders of
Wales, which I have hurried to from the circuit
in order to pass a week with my sister.   She
has lately come hither for the sake of her
children's breathing the pure air which blows
from the Welsh mountains, and enjoying the
pleasures which this beautiful country affords.
It is the most beautiful country that I have
seen in England, or anywhere else, except in
Switzerland; indeed, it very much resembles

some parts of Switzerland, but every thing is
on a smaller scale; the mountains are less high,
the rocks less craggy, and the torrents less
rapid.   The valleys are perfectly Swiss, and
are enchanting: scattered over with villages
and farm-houses, and portioned out into a
multitude of small fields, they bespeak a happy
equality of property, and transport one back in
idea to the infancy of society. . . . But the
most beautiful objects in this country, and
which are in a great degree independent of the
season, are the health, the cheerfulness, and
the contentment which appear on the countenances of the inhabitants.

The poor people here have a custom which
I never knew observed anywhere else, and
which is very poetical, and very affecting.
Once a year (on Palm Sunday) they get up
early in the morning, and gather the violets
and primroses, and the few other flowers which
at this season are to be found in the fields, and
with their little harvest they hasten to the
churchyard and strew the flowers over the
graves of their nearest relations. Some arrange
their humble tribute of affection in different
forms with a great deal of taste.   The young

girls who are so fortunate as never to have lost
any near relation or any friend, exert themselves that the tombs of the strangers who have
died in the village, at a distance from all who
knew them, may not be left unhonored ; and
hardly a grave appears without some of these
affectionate ornaments. I came here soon after
this ceremony had been observed, and was surprised, on walking through a churchyard, to
find in it the appearance of a garden; and to
see the flowers withering, each in the place in
which it had been fixed. . . .

———

LADY SYDNEY OWENSON MORGAN TO HER SISTER.

LAKE OF COMO, June 26, 1819.

. . . We had been offered the use of two
beautiful villas on the Lake of Como for nothing ; one of them, the Villa Someriva, one of
the handsomest palaces in Lombardy. We left
Milan ten days back, and have since lived in a
state of enchantment, and I really believe in
fairy-land. I know not where to refer you for
an account of the Lake of Como except to
" Lady M. W. Montagu's Letters." The lake is
fifty miles long, and the stupendous and magnificent mountains which embosom it are strewn

along their edges with the fantastic villas of the nobility of Milan, to which, as there is no road, there is no approach but by water. We took boat at the pretty, antique town of Como, and literally landed in the drawing-room of the Villa Tempi. The first things I perceived were the orange and lemon trees, laden with fruit, growing in groves in the open air; the American aloes, olive trees, vines, and mulberries, all in blossom or fruit, covering the mountains almost to their summits. The blossoms and orange-flowers, with the profusion of roses and wild pinks, were almost too intoxicating for our vulgar senses.

The next day we set off on our aquatic excursions through regions the mildest, the lovliest, the most romantic that can be conceived. We landed at all the curious and classical points—at Pliny's fountain, the site of his villa, etc., and after a course of twenty-five miles reached *my villa* of Someriva, which we found to be a splendid palace, all marble, surrounded by groves of orange-trees, but so vast, so solitary, so imposing, and so remote from all medical aid, that I gave up the idea of occupying it, and rowed off to visit other villas, and at last set up our boat at a pretty inn on the lake, where we sat up half the night watching the arrival of boats and listening to the choruses of the boatmen. The next day we returned, and after new voyages found a beautiful little villa on the lake, ten minutes' row from Como, which we have taken for two months, at six pounds a month. The Villa Fontana consists of two pavilions, as they are called here, or small houses of two stories, which are separated by a garden. In one reside the Signor and Signora, our hosts, with a charming family; in the other reside the Signor and Signora Morgan, with an Italian *valet-de-chambre*. These pavilions are on the lake in a little pyramid, the vines and grapes festooned from tree to tree, and woven into a canopy above. The lake spreads before us with all its mountain beauties and windings. To the right lies the town of Como, with its Gothic cathedral. Immediately behind us, on every side, rise the mountains which divide Italian Switzerland from Lombardy, covered with vines, olives, and lime-trees, and all this is lighted by a brilliant sun and canopied by skies bright, and blue, and cloudless. We have already made some excursions into these enchanting mountains, which are like cultivated gardens raised into the air, and walked within a mile of the Swiss frontier. We have a boat belonging to the villa anchored in the garden, in which we jump and row off. But of all the delights, imagine that shoals of foolish fish float on the surface of the lake in the evening, and that Morgan, who ambitioned nothing but a nibble on the Liffey line, here catches the victims of his art by dozens! Our villa consists of seven pretty rooms on the upper floor, and four below. The floors are stone, sprinkled with water two or three times a day; the walls painted in fresco, green jalousies, and muslin draperies, and yet, with all these cooling precautions, the heat obliges us to sit still all day. There is only one circumstance that reconciles me to your not sharing our pleasures, and that is a small matter of thunder and lightning, which comes about two days out of three, and is sometimes a little too near and too loud for the nerves of some of my friends. At this present moment it shakes the house, and the rain is falling as if Cox of Kilkenny was coming again. . . . Morgan is making great progress on the guitar. I think it would amuse you to witness the life we lead here. We rise early, and as our house is a perfect smother, we open the blinds (the sashes are never shut) and paradise bursts on us with a sun and sky that you never dreamt of in your philosophy. We breakfast under our arcade of vines, and the table is covered with peaches and nectarines, while the fish literally pop their heads out of the lake to be fed, though Morgan, like a traitor, takes them by hundreds. Except you saw him in a yellow muslin gown and straw hat, on the Lake of Como, you have no idea of human felicity! All day we are shut up in our respective little studies, in which the light scarcely penetrates, for the intolerable heat obliges every one to remain shut up during the middle of the day, and the houses and villages look as if they were uninhabited. At two o'clock we dine, at five, drink tea, and then we are off to the mountains, and frequently don't come back till night, or else we are on the lake; but in either instance we are in scenes which no pencil could delineate, nor pen describe. The mountains with their valleys and glens are covered with fig-trees, chestnuts, and olive-trees, and with the

lovely vineyards which are formed into festoons and arcades, and have quite another appearance from the stunted vineyards of France.
The other day, after dinner, we walked on till
we came to some barriers, where we were
stopped by *douaniers.* We asked where we
were, and found it was Switzerland. So, having walked through a pretty Swiss village,
and admired a sign " William Tell," we walked
back to Italy to tea. . . .

LADY MARY WORTLEY MONTAGU TO HER DAUGH-
TER THE COUNTESS OF BUTE.

LOUVERE, July 10, 1753.

. . . I have been these six weeks, and still
am, at my dairy-house, which joins to my garden. I believe I have already told you it is a
long mile from the castle, which is situate in
the midst of a very large village, once a considerable town, part of the walls still remaining,
and has not vacant ground enough about it to
make a garden, which is my greatest amusement, it being troublesome now to walk, or
even to go in the chaise till the evening. I
have fitted up in this farm-house a room for
myself, that is to say, strewed the floor with
rushes, covered the chimney with moss and

branches, and adorned the room with basins of earthen ware (which is made here to great perfection) filled with flowers, and put in some straw chairs, and a couch bed, which is my whole furniture. This spot of ground is so beautiful, I am afraid you will scarce credit the description, which, however, I can assure you, shall be very literal, without any embellishment from imagination. It is on a bank, forming a kind of peninsula, raised from the river Oglio fifty feet, to which you may descend by easy stairs cut in the turf, and either take the air on the river, which is as large as the Thames at Richmond, or by walking an avenue two hundred yards on the side of it, you find a wood of a hundred acres, which was already cut into walks and ridings when I took it. I have only added fifteen bowers in different views, with seats of turf. They were easily made, here being a large quantity of underwood, and a great number of wild vines, which twist to the top of the highest trees, and from which they make a very good sort of wine they call *Brusco*. I am now writing to you in one of these arbors, which is so thick shaded, the sun is not troublesome, even at noon. Another is on the side of the river, where I have made a camp kitchen, that I may take the fish, dress, and eat it immediately, at the same time see the barks, which ascend or descend every day to or from Mantua, Guastalla, or Pont de Vie, all considerable towns. This little wood is carpeted in their succeeding seasons with violets and strawberries, inhabited by a nation of nightingales, and filled with game of all kinds, excepting deer and wild boar, the first being unknown here, and not being large enough for the other.

. . . My garden was a plain vineyard when it came into my hands not two years ago, and it is, with a small expense, turned into a garden that (apart from the advantage of the climate) I like better than that of Kensington. The Italian vineyards are not planted like those in France, but in clumps, fastened to trees planted in equal ranks (commonly fruit trees), and continued in festoons from one to another, which I have turned into covered galleries of shade, that I can walk in the heat without being incommoded by it. I have made a dining-room of verdure, capable of holding a table of twenty covers; the whole ground is three hundred and seventeen feet in length,

and two hundred in breadth. You see it is
far from large ; but so prettily disposed (though
I say it), that I never saw a more agreeable
rustic garden, abounding with all sorts of fruit,
and producing a variety of wines. I would
send you a pipe, if I did not fear the customs
would make you pay too dear for it. I believe
my description gives you but an imperfect idea
of my garden. Perhaps I shall succeed better
in describing my manner of life, which is as
regular as that of any monastery. I generally
rise at six, and as soon as I have breakfasted,
put myself at the head of my needle-women
and work with them till nine. I then inspect
my dairy, and take a turn among my poultry,
which is a very large inquiry. I have, at present, two hundred chickens, besides turkeys,
geese, ducks, and peacocks. All things have
hitherto prospered under my care ; my bees
and silk-worms are doubled, and I am told that,
without accidents, my capital will be so in two
years' time. At eleven o'clock I retire to my
books, I dare not indulge myself in that pleasure above an hour. At twelve I constantly
dine, and sleep after dinner till about three. I
then send for some of my old priests, and

either play at piquet or whist, till 't is cool enough to go out. One evening I walk in my wood, where I often sup, take the air on horse-back the next, and go on the water the third. The fishery on this part of the water belongs to me ; and my fisherman's little boat (to which I have a green lutestring awning) serves me for a barge. He and his son are my rowers without any expense, he being very well paid by the profit of the fish, which I give him on condi-tion of having every day one dish for my table. Here is plenty of every sort of fresh-water fish (excepting salmon), but we have a large trout so like it, that I, who have almost forgot the taste, do not distinguish it. . . .

MRS. MARY DELANY TO MRS. DEWES.

DELVILLE, June 22, 1750.

My garden is at present in the high glow of beauty, my cherries ripening, roses, jessamine, and pinks in full bloom, and the hay partly spread and partly in cocks—complete the rural scene. We have discovered a new breakfasting place under the shade of nut-trees, impenetra-ble to the sun's rays, in the midst of a grove of elms, where we shall breakfast this morning ; I

have ordered cherries, strawberries, and nosegays to be laid on our breakfast-table, and have
appointed a harper to be here to play to us during our repast, who is to be hid among the trees.
Mrs. Hamilton is to breakfast with us, and is to
be cunningly led to this place *and surprised.* . . .

Last Sunday I had a good deal of company.
Monday, *dined* in my garden—the Vesey family with us.   In the afternoon drank tea in my
orangerie ; company after company till nine at
night. . . . Thursday, dined at Mr. Franklin's;
Friday, spent the whole day without any inter-
ruption at home—worked, walked, talked till
dinner, and sat quiet, listening to the harper till
six ; then picked roses—three baskets full.   At
seven, drank tea in the orangerie ; then walked
all over our meadows, fed our deer, saw two
beautiful fawns and the two young favorite
coach-horses eat their oats in the field ; stood
by whilst the cows were milking, till it grew so
late that we thought it prudent to come home,
and I hastened to my closet to finish this letter,
because to-morrow we spend at Lucan, and are
to call Mrs. Hamilton at eight, who goes with
us, and I shall not have a moment of the day
to myself.   Thus having given you, my dearest

sister, an account of what I have done and what I am to do, I retire, wishing you a good-night.

WILLIAM COWPER TO JOHN NEWTON.

OLNEY, September 18, 1784.

. . . My greenhouse is never so pleasant as when we are just upon the point of being turned out of it. The gentleness of the autumnal suns, and the calmness of this latter season, make it a much more agreeable retreat than we ever find it in summer; when, the winds being generally brisk, we cannot cool it by admitting a sufficient quantity of air, without being at the same time incommoded by it. But now I sit with all the windows and the door wide open, and am regaled with the scent of every flower in a garden as full of flowers as I have known how to make it. We keep no bees, but if I lived in a hive I should hardly hear more of their music. All the bees in the neighborhood resort to a bed of mignonette, opposite to the window, and pay me for the honey they get out of it by a hum, which, though rather monotonous, is as agreeable to my ear as the whistling of my linnets. All the sounds that nature utters are delightful—at least in this country. I should not perhaps find the roaring of lions in Africa, or of bears in Russia, very pleasing ; but I know no beast in England whose voice I do not account musical, save and except always the braying of an ass. The notes of all our birds and fowls please me, without one exception. I should not indeed think of keeping a goose in a cage, that I might hang him up in the parlor for the sake of his melody, but a goose upon a common, or in a farm-yard, is no bad performer ; and as to insects, if the black beetle, and beetles indeed of all hues, will keep out of my way, I have no objection to any of the rest ; on the contrary, in whatever key they sing, from the gnat's fine treble to the bass of the bumble bee, I admire them all. . . .

MISS MARY RUSSELL MITFORD TO MISS EMILY JOPH-
SON.

THREE-MILE CROSS, April 27, 1842.

. . . Well, perhaps if I could be all the time I covet, among the sweet flowers and the fresh grass, I should not enjoy as I do the brief intervals into which I do contrive to concentrate so much childish felicity. Who is it that talks

of " the cowslip vales of England ? " Is it you,
my beloved ? The words are most true and
most dear. Oh ! how I love those meadows,
yellow with cowslips and primroses ; those
winding brooks, or rather *that* winding brook,
golden with the water ranunculus ; those Silchester coppices, clothed with wood-sorrel,
wood-anemone, wild hyacinth, and primroses
in clusters as large as the table at which I
write ! I do not love musk—almost the only
odor called sweet that I do not love ; yet coming this evening on the night-scented odora
with its beautiful green cups, I almost loved
the scent for the form in which it grew. But
the cowslips, the wild hyacinths, the primroses,
the violet—oh ! what scent may match with
theirs ? I try to like the garden, but my heart
is in the fields and woods. I have been in the
meadows to-night. I ran away, leaving my father asleep. I could not help it. And oh, what
a three hours of enjoyment we had—Flush, and
the puppies, and I !—I myself, I verily believe,
the youngest-hearted of all. Then I have been
to Silchester too. My father went there ; and
I got out and ran round the walls and coppices
one way, as he drove the other. How grateful

I am to that gracious Providence, who makes
the most intense enjoyment the cheapest and
the commonest! I do love the woods and
fields! Oh! surely all the stars under the sun,
even if they were brighter than those earthly
stars ever seem to me, could not compare with
the green grass and the sweet flowers of this
delicious season!

I mistrust the feeling of poetry of all those
who consent to pass the spring amongst brick
walls, when they might come and saunter
amongst lanes and coppices. To live in the
country is, in my mind, to bring the poetry of
Nature home to the eyes and heart. And how
can those who do love the country talk of autumn as rivalling the beauty of spring? Only
look at the texture of the young leaves; see
the sap mounting into the transparent twigs as
you stand under an oak; feel the delicious
buds; inhale the fragrance of bough and herb,
of leaf and flower; listen to the birds and the
happy insects; feel the fresh balmy air. This is a
rhapsody; but I have no one to whom to talk,
for if I mention it to my father, he talks of
" my killing myself "; as if that which is balm
and renovation were poison and suicide. . . .

FRANCIS JEFFREY TO CHARLES WILKES.

CRAIGCROOK, March 28, 1830.

I never saw three such days in March. To be sure, they are the first days of my vacation, and come after a hard winter of work and weather. But they have been so deliciously soft, so divinely calm and bright, and the grass is so green, and the pale-blue sky so resonant with larks in the morning, and the loud, strong bridal chuckle of blackbirds and thrushes at sunset, and the air so lovesick with sweetbrier, and the garden so bright with hepaticas, and primroses, and violets, and my transplanted trees dancing out so gracefully from my broken clumps, and my leisurely evenings wearing away so tranquilly, that they have passed in a sort of enchantment, to which I scarcely remember any thing exactly parallel since I first left college in the same sweet season to meditate on my first love, in my first ramble in the Highlands.

Well, it is a fine thing, this spring, especially when it comes with the healing of leisure on its wings, and after a long, dark season of labor, and winter, and weariness. . . .

OUT-OF-DOORS.

CHARLES ARMITAGE BROWN TO CHARLES WENT-
WORTH DILKE.

INVERNESS, August 7, 1818.

What shall I write about? I am resolved to
send you a letter, but where is the subject? I
have already stumped away on my ten toes six
hundred and forty-two miles, and seen many fine
sights, but I am puzzled to know what to make
choice of. Suppose I begin with myself; there
must be a pleasure in that; and, by way of variety, I must bring in Mr. Keats. Then, be it
known, in the first place, we are in as continued
a bustle as an old dowager at home—always
moving—moving from one place to another,
like Dante's inhabitants of the Sulphur Kingdom in search of cold ground—prosing over
the map, calculating distances, packing up
knapsacks, and paying bills. There 's so much
for yourself, my dear. " Thank ye, sir." How
many miles to the next town? " Seventeen
lucky miles, sir." That must be at least twenty;

come along, Keats; here 's your stick; why, we forgot the map! now for it; seventeen lucky miles! I must have another hole taken up in the strap of my knapsack. Oh, the misery of coming to the meeting of three roads without a finger-post! There 's an old woman coming; God bless her! she 'll tell us all about it. Eh! she can't speak English! Repeat the name of the town over in all ways, but the true spelling way, and possibly she may understand. No, we have not got the brogue. Then toss up heads or tails, for right and left, and fortune send us the right road! Here 's a soaking shower coming! ecod! it rolls between the mountains as if it would drown us. At last we come, wet and weary, to the long-wished-for inn. What have you for dinner? "Truly nothing." No eggs? "We have two." Any loaf-bread? "No, sir, but we 've nice oat-cakes." Any bacon? any dried fish? "No, no, no, sir!" But you 've plenty of whiskey? "Oh, yes, sir; plenty of whiskey!" This is melancholy. Why should so beautiful a country be poor? Why can't craggy mountains and granite rocks bear corn, wine, and oil? These are our misfortunes; these are what

make me " an eagle's talon in the waist." But
I am well repaid for my sufferings. We came
out to endure, and to be gratified with scenery,
and lo ! we have not been disappointed either
way. As for the oat-cakes, I was once in despair about them. I was not only too dainty,
but they absolutely made me sick. With a
little gulping I can manage them now. Mr.
Keats, however, is too unwell for fatigue and
privation. I am waiting here to see him off in
the smack for London. . . .

JOHN KEATS TO THOMAS KEATS.

LETTER FINDLAY, August 3, 1818.

We have made but poor progress lately,
chiefly from bad weather, for my throat is in a
fair way of getting well, so I have had nothing
of consequence to tell you till yesterday, when
we went up Ben Nevis, the highest mountain
in Great Britain. On that account I will never
ascend another in this empire — Skiddaw is
nothing to it either in height or difficulty. It
is above 4,300 feet from the sea level, and Fort-
William stands at the head of a salt-water lake,
consequently we took it completely from that
level. I am heartily glad it is done—it is

almost like a fly crawling up a wainscote. Imagine the task of mounting ten Saint Pauls without the convenience of staircases. We set out about five in the morning with a guide in the tartan and cap, and soon arrived at the foot of the first ascent which we immediately began upon—after much fag and tug and a rest and a glass of whiskey apiece we gained the top of the first rise and saw then a tremendous chap above us, which, the guide said, was still far from the top. After the first rise our way lay along a heath valley in which there was a loch ; after about a mile in this valley we began our next ascent, more formidable by far than the last, and kept mounting with short intervals of rest until we got above all vegetation, among nothing but loose stones which lasted us to the very top. The guide said we had three miles of a stony ascent. We gained the first tolerable level after the valley to the height of what in the valley we had thought the top, and saw still above us another huge crag which still the guide said was not the top. To that we made with an obstinate fag, and having gained it, there came on a mist. The whole immense head of the mountain is composed of large loose stones—thousands of acres. Before we had got half-way up we passed large patches of snow, and near the top there is a chasm some hundred feet deep completely glutted with it. Talking of chasms, they are the finest wonder of the whole—they appear great rents in the very heart of the mountain, though they are not, being at the side of it, but other huge crags arising round it give the appearance to Nevis of a shattered heart or core in itself. These chasms are 1,500 feet in depth, and are the most tremendous places I have ever seen—they turn one giddy if you choose to give way to it. We tumbled in large stones and set the echoes at work in fine style. Sometimes these chasms are tolerably clear, sometimes there is a misty cloud which seems to steam up, and sometimes they are entirely smothered with clouds.

After a little time the mist cleared away, but still there were large clouds about, attracted by old Ben to a certain distance, so as to form as it appeared large dome curtains which kept sailing about, opening and shutting at intervals here and there and everywhere ; so that, although we did not see one vast wide extent of prospect all round, we saw something perhaps finer—these cloud-veils opening with a dissolving motion and showing us the mountainous region beneath as through a loophole— these cloudy loopholes ever varying and discovering fresh prospect east, west, north, and south. Then it was misty again, and again it was fair—then puff came a cold breeze of wind and bared a craggy chap we had not yet seen, though in close neighborhood. Every now and then we had overhead clear blue sky and the sun pretty warm. I do not know whether I can give you an idea of the prospect from a large mountain top. You are on a stony plain which of course makes you forget you are on any but low ground—the horizon or rather edges of this plain being above 4,000 feet above the sea, hide all the country immediately beneath you, so that the next object you see all round next to the edges of the flat top are the summits of mountains some distance off. As you move about on all sides you see more or less of the near neighbor country according as the mountain you stand upon is in different parts deep or rounded. But the most new thing of all is the sudden leap of the

eye from the extremity of what appears a plain
into so vast a distance. On one part of the
top there is a handsome pile of stones done
pointedly by some soldiers of artillery; I
climbed on to them and so got a little higher
than old Ben himself. . . .

FRANCIS JEFFREY TO CHARLES WILKES.

TARBET, August 5, 1818.

Here we are in a little inn on the banks of
Loch Lomond, in the midst of the mists of the
mountains, the lakes, heaths, rocks, and cascades which have been my passion since I
was a boy; and to which, like a boy, I have run
away the instant I could get my hands clear of
law, and review, and Edinburgh. We have been
here for four days, and Charlotte is at least as
much enchanted with the life we lead as I am;
and yet it is not a life that most ladies with a
spark of *fineness* in them would think very delightful. They have no post-horses in the Highlands, and we sent away those that brought us
here, with orders to come back for us to-morrow, and so we are left without a servant, entirely at the mercy of the natives. The first
day we walked about ten miles over wet heath

and slippery rocks, and sailed five or six on the
lake in a steamboat, which surprised us as we
were sitting in a lonely wild little bay, shel-
tering ourselves from a summer shower under a
hanging copse. It is a new experiment that
for the temptation of tourists. It circumnavi-
gates the whole lake every day in about ten
hours; and it was certainly very strange and
striking to hear and see it hissing and roaring
past the headlands of our little bay, foaming
and spouting like an angry whale; but, on the
whole, I think it rather vulgarizes the scene
too much, and I am glad it is found not to answer, and is to be dropped next year. Well,
then, the day after, we lounged about an hour
or two in the morning, then skimmed across
the lake in a little skiff, and took to climbing
up the hill in good earnest. This, I assure you,
is no fine lady's work. It is 3,400 feet high, with
an ascent of near five miles, very rough, wet,
and rocky in many places; and Charley had
fine slipping, and stumbling, and puffing, before she got to the top. However, by the help
of the guide's whiskey and my own, she got
through very safe and proud at last. For more
than 2,000 feet the air was quite clear, but a

thick fog rested on the top, and but for the glory of the thing, we might have stopped where it began. The prospect, however, became very grand and singular before it was quite swallowed up. The whole landscape took a strange silvery skyish tint, from the thin veil of vapor in which it began to sink; and some distant mountains, on which the sun continued to shine, assumed the most delicate and tender green color you ever saw, while the water of the lake, with all its islands, seemed lifted up to the level of the eye, and the whole scene to be wavering in the skies, like what is described of the *fata morgana* in Sicily. We all fell twenty times in our descent, and were completely besmeared with mud, which was partly washed away by a fine milky shower which fell upon us as we again crossed over in our boat. The day after, we walked good twelve miles before dinner, up to the wildest and least frequented end of the lake, making various detours, and discovering at every turn the most enchanting views and recesses. In the evening we rowed down the smooth glassy margin of the water to a gentleman's house a mile or two off, and walked home in the twilight. . . .

CHARLES KINGSLEY TO HIS WIFE.

PEN-Y-GWRYD, August, 1856.

I have had, as far as scenery is concerned, the finest day I ever had. We started for Edno at 10, but did not find it till 2, because we mistook the directions, and walked from 10 till 1.30 over a Steinerer Maar, a sea of syenite and metamorphic slate which baffles all description, 2,000 feet above Gwynant, ribs and peaks and walls of rock leaping up and rushing down, average 50 to 100 feet, covered with fir, club moss, crowberry and bearberry, and ling, of course. Over these we had to scramble up and down, beating for Edno Lake as you would beat for a partridge, but in vain. All we found was one old cock grouse, who went off hollowing " Cock-cock-what-a-shame cock-cock," till we were fairly beat. In despair we made, not a dash, but a crawl, at Moel Meirch ("Margaret's Peak," some pathetic story I suppose), which rises about 100 feet above the stony sea, a smooth pyramid of sandy-pink syenite. Hughes got up first, by a crack, for the walls are like china, and gave a who-whoop ; there was Edno half a mile beyond, and only a valley as deep as from Finchamstead church to the river to

cross, besides a few climbs of 50 feet. So there
we got, and ate our hard-boiled eggs and drank
our beer, and then set to, and caught just nothing. The fish, always sulky and capricious,
would not stir. But the delight of being there
again, 2,200 feet up, out of the sound of aught
but the rush of wind and water and the whistle
of the sheep (which is just like a penny whistle
ill-blown), and finding one's self *at home* there!
Every rock, even the steps of slate and foot-
holds of grass which ———— and I used to use,
just the same. Unchanged forever. It is an
awful thought. Soon we found out why the fish
would n't rise. The cloud which had been
hanging on Snowdon, lowered. Hebog and
Cnicht caught it. It began to roll up from the
sea in great cabbage-headed masses, grew as
dark as twilight. The wind rolled the lake into
foam; we staggered back to an old cave, where
we shall sleep, please God, ere we come home,
and then the cloud lowered, the lake racing
along in fantastic flakes, and heaps of white
steam hiding every thing 50 yards off one minute, then leaving all clear and sharp-cut pink
and green. While out of it came a rain of
marbles and Minie bullets—a rain which

searches, and drenches, and drills. Luckily I had on a flannel shirt. We waited as long as we dared, and then steered home by compass, for we could not see 50 yards, except great rows of giants in the fog, sitting humped up side by side, like the ghosts of the sons of Anak staring into the bogs. So home we went, floundering through morass and scrambling up and down the giants, which were crags 50 to 100 feet high, for we dared not pick our road for fear of losing our bearings by compass. And we were wet—oh, were we not wet? but as a make-weight, we found the "Grass of Parnassus" in plenty, and as we coasted the vale of Gwynant, 1,500 feet up, the sight of Snowdon, sometimes through great gaps of cloud, sometimes altogether hidden, the lights upon that glorious vista of Gwynant and Dinas, right down to Hebog—the flakes of cloud rushing up the vale of Gwynant far below us—no tongue can describe it. . . .

LORD EDWARD FITZGERALD TO HIS MOTHER.

Sᴛ. Aɴɴ's, Nᴇᴡ Bʀᴜɴsᴡɪᴄᴋ, August 16, 1788.

. . . I do sincerely long to see you; I think if I could carry you here, I should live tolerably happy. There is certainly something in a military life that excites and keeps up one's spirits. I feel exactly like my uncle Toby at the sound of a drum, and the more I hear it the more I like it ; there is a mixture, too, of country life and military life here that is pleasant. I have got a garden for the soldiers which employs me a great deal. I flatter myself next year that it will furnish the men with quantities of vegetables, which will be of great service to them. Another of my amusements is my canoe ; I have already had two expeditions in it. I and another officer went up the river in her for thirty miles; we stayed two days, and had our provisions and blankets with us, and slept in the woods ; one of the nights, cooked our victuals, and did every thing ourselves.

It is very pleasant here sometimes to go in this way exploring, ascending far up some river or creek, and finding sometimes the finest lands and most beautiful spots in nature, which are not at all known, and quite wild. As soon as our review is over, I am to go on one of these parties, up a river, the source and course of which is yet unknown. There is a great convenience in the canoes, they are so light, two men can carry them easily on their shoulders, so that you go from river to river without any trouble : it is the only method of travelling in this country. A canoe here is like a postchaise at home, and the rivers and lakes your post-horses. You would laugh to see the faithful Tony and I carrying one. . . .

LORD EDWARD FITZGERALD TO HIS MOTHER.

NEW BRUNSWICK, November 21, 1788.

. . . I will now give you some account of myself, *what* I do, and *how* I do. Our winter is quite set in, and the river frozen over, and I am skating from morning till night. I don't know how long the rage will last, but while it does, it is very pleasant. I begin in the morning as soon as it is light, stay till breakfast, go out, and stay again till it is time to dress and parade. Luckily, I have no other necessary business now, for our drilling is over till spring, except twice a week taking a good long march ; the snow, I believe, will soon stop that, and then I mean to go to Quebec in snow-shoes. I believe I shall be out most of the winter. I have two or three hunting parties to go on, and they sel-dom last longer than a fortnight ; these, and my journey to Quebec, and some excursions from thence, will take up most of my winter. I long to give you an account of some of my trips; the idea of being out-of-doors, notwithstanding the inclemency of the weather, and of overcoming all the difficulties of nature, by the ingenuity of man, delights me. Everybody who has tried this says it is much the warmest way of living in winter; for, by being in the woods, you are sheltered from the winds; and, at night, by clearing away the snow, banking it up round, and in the middle of the space making a large fire, you are much warmer than in the best house. This is what I hear.

You may guess how eager I am to try if I like the woods in winter as well as in summer. I believe I shall never again be prevailed on to live in a house. I long to teach you all how to make a good spruce bed. Three of the coldest nights we have had yet, I slept in the woods with only one blanket, and was just as comfortable as in a room. It was in a party with Gen. Carleton; we went about twenty miles from this to look at a fine tract of land that had been passed over in winter. You may guess how I enjoyed this expedition, being where, in all probability, there had never been but one per-

son before ; we struck the land the first night
and lay there ; we spent three days afterwards
in going over it. It will be now soon settled.
I cannot describe all the feelings one has in
these excursions, when one wakens,—perhaps
in the middle of the night, in a fine open forest,
all your companions snoring about you, the
moon shining through the trees, the burning of
the fire,—in short, every thing strikes you.
Dearest, dearest mother, how I have thought
of you at those times, and of all at dear Fres-
cati ! and after being tired of thinking, lying
down like a dog, and falling asleep till day-
break ; then getting up, no dressing, or cloth-
ing, or trouble, but just giving one's self a
shake, and away to the spring to wash one's
face. I have had two parties with the savages
which are still pleasanter—you may guess the
reason,—there are *des dames* who are the most
comical creatures in the world.

LORD EDWARD FITZGERALD TO HIS MOTHER.

QUEBEC, March 14, 1789.

. . . The hours here are a little inconvenient to us as yet ; whenever we wake at night,
we want to eat, the same as in the woods, and

as soon as we eat, we want to sleep. In our journey we were always up two hours before day, to load and get ready to march; we used to stop between three and four, and it generally took us from that till night to shovel out the snow, cut wood, cook, and get ready for night; so that immediately after our suppers, we were asleep, and whenever any one wakes in the night he puts some wood on the fire, and eats a bit before he lies down again; but for my part I was not much troubled with waking in the night.

I really do think there is no luxury equal to that of lying before a good fire on a good spruce bed, after a good supper, and a hard moose chase in a fine clear frosty moonlight starry night. But to enter into the spirit of this, you must understand what a moose chase is. The man himself runs the moose down by pursu-ing the *track*. Your success in killing depends on the number of people you have to pursue and relieve one another in going first (which is the fatiguing part of snow-shoeing), and on the depth and hardness of the snow; for when the snow is hard, and has a crust, the moose cannot get on, as it cuts his legs, and then he stops to make battle. But when the snow is soft, though it be above his belly, he will go on, three, four, or five days, for then the man cannot get on so fast, as the snow is heavy, and he only gets his game by perseverance,—an Indian never gives him up. . . .

MISS ELIZABETH CARTER TO MISS CATHERINE TALBOT.

DEAL, July 13, 1750.

. . . My dear children keep me in pretty constant employ till three o'clock, and this fine weather we usually form some party for the afternoon. You cannot imagine what odd, good-humored, sociable kind of things these parties of ours are, which give us a very complete enjoyment of this charming country, as most of us are good walkers, and have no objection to the full blaze of July. However, there is always a led chariot, to which no mortal is constant but Mr. Burton, who is too fat and too lazy ever to walk, and too good-natured not to suffer very quietly the being squeezed to death as often as any of the company happen to grow weary, whom he takes up by twos and threes, and, as soon as they are tired, takes up a new succession. We generally drink tea in some village or at a lone farm-house, and by this method of rambling discover a thousand beauties which would be unobserved in a more regular scheme. . . .

―――――

CHARLES JAMES MATHEWS TO HIS MOTHER.

NAPLES, May 6, 1824.

. . . Since last week we have had the regular Italian weather, though till now it has occasionally been stormy and bad. The month of March is the worst in the year, and April little better, but May, I think, must be the most delightful of the whole twelve, as the flies and mosquitoes have not yet begun to bite, and there is generally a refreshing wind. I have enjoyed myself most particularly this week, and in a manner you little think of, for, wonderful to relate, I have taken to walking, for the first time in my life, and enjoy it more than any other mode of travelling. On Monday last I got up at four o'clock, and, strapping on my knapsack (a most convenient little one that Lord B. gave me for Pompeii), I set off in full costume, with my collar on my shoulders open and cool, my linen gaiters and travelling cap, and gayly trudged on to Pozzuoli. There I made a sketch of the Temple of Serapis, which, having finished, and without being bored with the attentions of a cicerone, I wandered about among the ancient tombs and palaces, of which there are so many remains at this interesting place, and then crossed the Solfatara, three miles of an extinguished volcano, walking on sulphur and brimstone still smoking, and then reached the Lake of Agnano, by whose shining and refreshing mirror I ate my bread and cheese and hard eggs, which I carried in my wallet, and enjoyed the glorious and matchless views under the cool shade of an olive tree. From hence I crossed gardens and orchards full of orange and lemon trees, from whose boughs I plucked as I pleased, and crossed from one mountain to another till I climbed the magnificent rock by which I arrived at Belvedere as the sun was setting, just in time to dress for dinner. You cannot imagine how delightful this ramble was, altogether about eighteen miles, not meeting a single soul except the peasants, whose good-humored countenances are always delightful. Whenever I passed through private orchards, there being no hedges, I saluted the farmers and thanked

them for their obliging courtesy in allowing me
such delicious rambles. This salute invariably
ended with an invitation to taste their wine,
and on entering the cottage (dirty enough)
cakes were produced, and excellent country
wine pledged round, the wives and daughters singing and dancing the Tarantella all
the time. This, by the bye, is the national
dance, and is said to be that which cures the
bite of the tarantula. The gayety of these
simple people is extraordinary. At parting
and following my road, a bunch of flowers is
presented and the rosy cheeks of the girls,
which I accepted and kissed with pleasure,
though to say the truth some of them smelt
fervidly of garlic. Nothing can be more delightful than these walks. . . .

THOMAS GUTHRIE TO G. M. TORRANCE.

KIRKTON, July 4, 1853.

This year we have done wonders with the
trolling tackle. Captain Stoddart caught an
$8\frac{1}{2}$ and two 7 lbs. trouts; and I, one 3 lbs.,
one $4\frac{1}{2}$ lbs., and another 7 lbs. weight. I was
rather proud of these achievements. The $4\frac{1}{2}$
lbs. one gave more sport than any of the rest,
and it needed both prompt and delicate management of rod and line to hold him fast; now

he was down to the black depths of the loch, then spinning away—my reel sounding the liveliest music to a fisher's ear—and by-and-by he was flinging himself bodily four or five feet out of the water.

But, four nights ago, I gained my greatest triumph. I was fishing for common trout with small loch hooks and a cast of my ordinary gut, when a hook—a small *green mantle* which I had dressed that day—was suddenly seized. There was a swirl, and then, to my amazement, away like lightning went the line from my whirling pirn. I was in a moment on my feet in the boat, crying to D——: "Row, it's a big fish, and my line will be out!" Well, there we were, backing, rowing, wheeling, and after some quarter of an hour's work or more, we neared the beach, where, leaping to shore, I drew to land a very fine 5 lbs. *salmo ferox*, which I despatched that night to Lord Panmure at Brechin. . . .

MISS MARY RUSSELL MITFORD TO BENJAMIN ROBERT HAYDON.

THREE-MILE CROSS, August 24, 1823.

Pray are you a cricketer? We are very great ones—I mean our parish, of which we—the feminine members—act audience, and "though we do not play, o'erlook" the balls. When I wrote to you last I was just going to see a grand match in a fine old park near us, Bramshill, between Hampshire, with Mr. Budd, and all England. I anticipated great pleasure from so grand an exhibition, and thought, like a simpleton, the better the play the more the enjoyment. Oh, what a mistake! There they were—a set of ugly old men, white-headed and bald-headed (for half of Lord's was engaged in the combat, players and gentlemen, Mr. Ward and Lord Frederick, the veterans of the green), dressed in tight white jackets (the Apollo Belvedere could not bear the hideous disguise of a cricket-jacket), with neckcloths primly tied round their throats, fine japanned shoes, silk stockings and gloves, instead of our fine village lads, with their unbuttoned collars, their loose waistcoats, and the large shirt-sleeves which give an air so picturesque and Italian to their glowing, bounding youthfulness;—there they stood, railed in by themselves, silent, solemn, slow; playing for money, making a business of the thing, grave as judges, taciturn as chess-players—a sort of dancers without music, instead of the glee, the fun, the shouts, the laughter, the glorious confusion of the country game.

And there we were, the lookers-on, in tents and
marquees, fine and freezing, dull as the players,
cold as this hard summer weather, shivering and
yawning and trying to seem pleased, the curse
of gentility on all our doings, as stupid as we
could have been in a ball-room.   I never was
so much disappointed in my life.   But every
thing is spoiled when money puts its ugly nose
in.   To think of playing cricket for hard cash !
Money and gentility would ruin any pastime
under the sun.   Much to my comfort (for the
degrading my favorite sport into a " science," as
they were pleased to call it, had made me quite
spiteful) the game ended unsatisfactorily to all
parties—winners and losers.   Old Lord Frederick, on some real or imaginary affront, took
himself off in the middle of the second innings,
so that the two last were played without him,
by which means his side lost, and the other
could hardly be said to win.   So be it always
when men make the noble game of cricket an
affair of bettings and hedgings, and maybe of
cheatings. . . .

WILLIAM HOWITT TO MISS MARY RUSSELL MITFORD.
NOTTINGHAM, September 10, 1835.

. . . Well, what do you think of our Nottingham men now ?   I shall send you a paper

to-morrow containing the account of the great cricket-match played here between Sussex and Nottingham. Perhaps you may have seen in the papers that the Nottingham club challenged the Sussex, and beat them about a fortnight ago at Brighton, and now they have beaten them again here. The match commenced on Monday, and was finished yesterday (Wednesday) at about half-past four o'clock. We wished you had been there—a more animated sight of the kind you never saw. On Sunday morning, as we were dressing, we saw a crowd going up the street, and immediately perceived that in the centre of it were the Sussex cricketers, arrived by the London coach, and going to the inn kept by one of our Nottingham cricketers. They looked exceedingly interesting, I assure you, being a set of very fine fellows, in their white hats, and with all their trunks, carpet-bags, and cloaks, coming, as we verily believed, to be beaten. Our interest was strongly excited, and on Monday morning we set off to the cricket-ground, which lies about a mile from the town, in the Forest, as it is still called, though not a tree is left upon it—a long, furzy common, crowned at the top with

about twenty windmills, and descending in a
steep slope to a fine level—round which the
race-course runs, and within the race-course lies
the cricket-ground, and the military ground for
the troop of horse which always occupy our
barracks. Each end of the cricket-ground was
completely enclosed by booths, and all up the
forest hill were scattered booths and tents with
flags flying, fires blazing, pots boiling, ale-bar-
rels standing, and carts and asses and people
bringing still more good things, ranged at the
farther side of the cricket-ground. I had the
strongest idea of an amphitheatre filled with
people that I ever had. In fact, it *was* an
amphitheatre. Along each side of the ground
ran a bank sloping down to it ; and it and the
tents and booths at the end were occupied with
a dense mass of people, and all up the hill
were groups, and on the race-stand an eager,
forward-leaning mass. There were said to be
twenty thousand people, all as silent as the
ground beneath them, except when some exploit of the players produced a sudden thunder
of applause. The playing was beautiful. Mr.
Ward, the late M.P. for the City of London,
came from the Isle of Wight to see the play,

and declared himself highly delighted. But nothing was so beautiful as the sudden shout and rush of the crowd when the last decisive notch was gained; to see the scorers suddenly snatch up their chairs, and run off with them towards the players' tent; to see the bat of Bart. Goode, the batsman on whom the fate of the game depended, spinning up in the air, where he had sent it in the ecstasy of the moment; and the crowd, that the instant before were as fixed and as silent as the earth itself, spread all over the green space, where the white figures of the players had till then been so gravely and, apparently, coolly contending—speeding with a murmur as of a sea, and over their heads, amid all the deafening clamor and confusion, the carrier-pigeon, with the red ribbon tied to its tail, the signal of loss or gain—I know not which—beating round and round, so as to ascertain its precise situation, and then flying off to bear the tidings to some strongly interested quarter. Was it not a beautiful sight? Should you not have been delighted to see it?

My thoughts on such occasions generally fly beyond the immediate place and time, and begin to contemplate consequences, and I could not help seeing what a wide difference twenty years has produced in the character of the English population. What a contrast is this play to bull-baiting, dog- and cock-fightings! So orderly, so manly, so generous in its character. It is the nearest approach to the athletic games of the Greeks that we have made, and the effect on the general mass of the people by the emulation it will excite must be excellent. There is something very beautiful in one distant county sending its peaceful champions to contend with those of another in a sport that has no drawback of cruelty or vulgarity in it, but has every recommendation of skill, taste, health, and generous rivalry. You, dear Miss Mitford, have done a great deal to promote this better spirit, and you could not have done more had you been haranguing Parliament, and bringing in bills for the purpose.

MISS MARY RUSSELL MITFORD TO MISS EMILY JEPHSON.

THREE-MILE-CROSS, October 30, 1829.

. . . Now, my dearest, I am going to tell you of an exploit of mine which I longed for you extremely to share. Last Saturday I dined out, and was reproached by a young fox-hunter with never having seen the hounds throw off. I said I should like the sight. The lady of the house said she would drive me some day. The conversation dropped, and I never expected to hear more of it. The next day, however, Sir John Cope (the master of the hounds) calling on my friend, the thing was mentioned and settled ; and the young man who originally suggested the matter rode over to let me know that at half-past nine the next day our friend would call for me. At half-past nine, accordingly, she came in a little limber pony-carriage, drawn by a high-blooded little mare, whom she herself (the daughter and sister of a whole race of fox-hunters) had been accustomed to hunt in Wiltshire, and attended by her husband's hunting-groom, excellently mounted.

The day was splendid, and off we set. It was the first day of the season. The hounds were to meet in Bramshill Park, Sir John Cope's old place ; and it was expected to be the greatest field and most remarkable day of many seasons. Mr. Warde, the celebrated fox-hunter,

—the very Nestor of the field, who, after keeping fox-hounds for fifty-seven years, has just,
at seventy-nine, found himself growing old and
given them up,—was on a visit at the house,
and all the hunt were likely to assemble to see
this delightful person ; certainly the pleasantest
old man that it ever has been my fortune to
foregather with—more beautiful than my father,
and in the same style.

Well off we set ; got to Bramshill just as
breakfast was over ; saw the hounds brought
out in front of the house ; drove to cover ; saw
the fox found, and the first grand burst at his
going off ; followed him to another covert, and
the scent being bad and the field so numerous,
that he was constantly headed back, both he,
who finally ran to earth, and another fox found
subsequently, kept dodging about from wood
to wood in that magnificent demesne—the very
perfection of park scenery, hill and dale, and
wood and water—and for about four hours we,
with our spirited pony, kept up with the chase,
driving about over road and no road, across
ditches and through gaps, often run away with,
sometimes almost tossed out, but with a degree
of delight and enjoyment such as I never felt

before, and never, I verily believe, shall feel again. The field (above a hundred horsemen, most of them the friends of my fair companion) were delighted with our sportsmanship, which in me was unexpected ; they showed us the kindest attention ; brought me the brush ; and when, at three o'clock, we and Mr. Warde and one or two others went in to luncheon, whilst the hounds went on to Eversley, I really do not believe that there was a gentleman present ungratified by our gratification. Unless you have seen such a scene, you can hardly imagine its animation or its beauty. The horses are most beautiful, and the dogs, although not pretty separately, are so when collected and in their own scenery ; which is also exactly the case with the fox-hunters' scarlet coats. . . .

MISS HANNAH MORE TO MISS ELIZABETH CARTER.

SANDLEFORD PRIORY, 1784.

. . . I have been such a stroller that I have hardly done so serious a thing as to write a letter during the whole bright and pleasant month of September. I spent that month at the house of a friend, in one of the most en-chanting vales of Somersetshire. The surround-

ing scenery was so lovely, so full of innocent
wildness, that I do not know any place that
ever caught such hold of my imagination. If
spring is the poet's season, it must be allowed
that autumn is the painter's. Such delicious
warmth in the coloring of the woods! Every
morning I rode through the most delightful
valleys, or crept along the sides of the most
beautiful hanging woods, where the blue smoke,
ascending from the cleanest white cottages in
the world, had the prettiest effect imaginable ;
it was a sort of thin gray ether, a kind of poetical smoke, which seemed too pretty to be
connected with the useful,—very unlike the
gross, substantial, culinary vapor, which suggests ideas only of corporeal and common
things. But most devoutly did I wish for you,
one day that I passed in a narrow and deep
valley, under a vast ledge of rocks, so lofty and
stupendous as to impress the mind with ideas
the most solemn and romantic. They were
shaped by nature into forms the most aston-
ishing and fantastic, exactly resembling Gothic
castles and ruined abbeys, which brought with
them a train of broken images, wild and amaz-
ing, or awful and affecting, as the scenes suc-

ceeded each other. But I was exceedingly
touched when, sitting down on a huge fragment
of rock, some of the company performed one of
Gray's wildest odes, in a style of taste and
feeling which made the happiest accompani-
ment imaginable to the scenery. . . .

MRS. SARA COLERIDGE TO AUBREY DE VERE.

HERNE BAY, September 18, 1849.

. . . Imagine us on our evening walk out
upon the East Cliff, a mile and a half from our
present abode. We have passed a rough path-
way, and, weary of a long, low hedge, the very
symbol of sameness and almost of nothingness,
have struck in by a breach which the sailors,
who sit there with their observatory telescopes,
have made upon the grassy cliff, and are looking upon the sea and sky and straggling town
of Herne Bay. The ruddy ball is sinking; over
it is a large feathery mass of cloudage that *was*
swan's-down, but now, thrilled through with
rosy light, resembles pinky crimson flames, and
the dark waters below are tinged with rose
color. In the distance appears the straggling
town, with its tall watch, or rather clock tower,
and its long pier, like a leviathan centipede,
walking out into the waves. This time we are

home before dark; another evening we set out later, and by the time we descend the cliff it is dark, and as we are pacing down the velvet path, as we call the smooth, grassy descent which leads to the town, there is Nurse in her black cloak waving in the wind, moving toward us through the dusk like a magnified bat. . . .

CHARLES DARWIN TO HIS WIFE.

MOOR PARK, April, 1858.

The weather is quite delicious. Yesterday, after writing to you, I strolled a little beyond the glade for an hour and a half, and enjoyed myself—the fresh yet dark-green of the grand Scotch firs, the brown of the catkins of the old birches, with their white stems, and a fringe of distant green from the larches made an excessively pretty view. At last I fell fast asleep on the grass, and awoke with a chorus of birds singing around me, and squirrels running up the trees, and some woodpeckers laughing, and it was as pleasant and rural a scene as ever I saw, and I did not care one penny how any of the beasts or birds had been formed. . . .

JAMES HOGG TO JOHN WILSON.

MOUNT BENGER, August, 1829.

MY DEAR AND HONORED JOHN:—I never thought you had been so unconscionable as to

desire a sportsman on the 11th or even the
13th of August to leave Ettrick Forrest for the
bare scraggy hills of Westmoreland !—Ettrick
Forest, where the black cocks and white cocks,
brown cocks and grey cocks, ducks, plovers and
peaseweeps and whilly-whaups are as thick as
the flocks that cover her mountains, and come
to the hills of Westmoreland that can nourish
nothing better than a castril or stonechat ! To
leave the great yellow-fin of Yarrow, or the still
larger grey-locher for the degenerate fry of
Troutbeck, Esthwaite, or even Westwater ! No,
no, the request will not do ; it is an unreasona-
ble one, and therefore not unlike yourself, for
besides, what would become of Old North and
Blackwood, and all our friends for game, were I
to come to Elleray just now ? I know of no
home of man where I could be so happy within
doors with so many lovely and joyous faces
around me ; but this is not the season for in-
door enjoyments ; they must be reaped on the
wastes among the blooming heath, by the silver
spring, or swathed in the delicious breeze of the
wilderness. Elleray, with all its sweets, could
never have been my choice for a habitation, and
perhaps you are the only Scottish gentleman

who ever made such a choice, and still persists in maintaining it, in spite of every disadvantage. Happy days to you and a safe return!

FRANCIS JEFFREY TO WILLIAM EMPSON.

KILLIN, August 2, 1834.

This is a great disappointment, and, after all, why were you so faint-hearted after coming so far? Rain! Oh effeminate cockney, and most credulous brother of a most unwise prognosticator of meteoric changes. Though it rained in the Bœotia of Yorkshire, must it rain also in the Attica of Argyll? Why, there has not been a drop of rain in the principality of Macallum-More for these ten days; but, on the contrary, such azure skies, and calm, cerulean waters, such love and laziness—inspiring heats by day, and such starlight rowings and walkings through fragrant live blossoms, and dewy birch woods by night; and then such glow-worms twinkling from tufts of heath and juniper, such naiads sporting on the white quartz pebbles, and meeting your plunges into every noon-day pool; and such herrings at breakfast, and haggises at dinner, and such pale, pea-green mountains, and a genuine Highland sacrament! The long sermon in Gaelic, preached out of tents to picturesque multitudes in the open air, grouped on rocks by the glittering sea, in one of the mountain bays of those long withdrawing lochs! You have no idea what you have missed; and for weather especially, there is no memory of so long a tract of calm, dry, hot weather at this season; and the fragrance of the mountain hay, and the continual tinkling of the bright waters! But you are not worthy even of the ideas of these things, and you shall have no more of them, but go unimproved to your den at Haileybury, or your stye at the Temple, and feed upon the vapor of your dungeon. When we found you had really gone back from your vow, we packed up for Loch Lomond yesterday, and came on here, where we shall stay in the good Breadalbane country till Monday. . . . And now it is so hot that I cannot write any more, but must go and cool myself in the grottoes to the rocky Dochart, or float under the deep shades of the translucent Lochy, or sit on the airy summit where the ruins of Finlairg catch the faint fluttering of the summer breeze. All Greek and Hebrew to you, only more melodious. Poor wretch! . . .

NORMAN MACLEOD TO JOHN MACKINTOSH.

DALKEITH, October, 1844.

"There is poetry in every thing." True, quite true, Emerson—thou true man, poet of the backwoods! But there is not poetry in a fishwife, surely? Surely there is; lots of it. Her creel has more than all Dugald Moore's tomes. Why there was one—I mean a fishwife—this moment in the lobby. She had a hooked nose. It seemed to be the type, nay the ancestor, of a cod-hook. Her mouth was a skate or turbot humanized; her teeth, selected from the finest oyster pearl; her eyes, whelks with the bonnets on—bait for old fish on sea or land; her hands and fingers in redness and toughness rivalled the crab, barring him of the Zodiac. Yet she was all poetry. I had been fagging, reading, and writing since 6 A.M. (on honor!)—had dived into Owen, was drowned in Edwards, and wrecked on Newman—my brain was wearied, when suddenly I heard the sound of "Flukes!" followed by "Had—dies!" (a name to which Haidee was as prose). I descended and gazed into the mysterious creel, and then came a gush of sunlight upon my spirit—visions of sunny mornings with winding shores, and clean, sandy, pearly beaches, and rippling waves glancing and glittering over white shells and polished stones, and breezy headlands ; and fishing-boats moving like shadows onward from the great deep ; and lobsters, and crabs, and spoutfish, and oysters, crawling, and chirping, and spouting out sea-water, the old " ocean gleaming like a silver shield." The fishwife was a Claude Lorraine ; her presence painted what did my soul good, and as her reward I gave her what I 'll wager never during her life had been given her before—all that she asked for her fish ! And why, you ask, have I sat down to write to you, beloved John, all this—to spend a sheet of paper, to pay one penny, to abuse ten tickings of my watch to write myself, like Dogberry, an ass? Why? " Nature," quoth d'Alembert, " puts questions which Nature cannot answer." And shall I beat Nature, and be able to answer questions put to me by John—Nature's own child? Be silent, and let neither of us shame our parent. Modesty forbids me to attempt any solution of thy question, dear John. Now for work. My pipe is out !

NORMAN MACLEOD TO HIS SISTER.

SHANDON, May, 1848.

I have been yearning here for quiet and retirement. I got it yesterday. I set off upon a steeple-chase, scenting like a wild ass the water from afar. But heather, birch, and the like, were my water in the desert. I found all. I passed through the upper park and entered a birch wood. I traced an old path, half trodden —whether by men or hares I could not tell. It led me to a wee burn. In a moment I found myself in the midst of a poem; one of those woodland lyrics which have a melody heard and unheard, which enters by the eye and ear, goes down to the heart, and steeps it in light, pours on it the oil of joy, and gives it "beauty for ashes." This same mountain spirit of a burn comes from the heather, from the lonely home of sheep, kites, and "peaseweeps." It enters a birch wood, and flows over the cleanest slate. When I met it, it was falling with a chuckling, gurgling laugh, into a small pool, clear as liquid diamond. The rock shelved over it and sheltered it. In the crevices of the rock were arranged, as tasteful nature alone can do, bunches of primroses, sprouting green ferns, and innumerable rock plants, while the sunlight gleaming from the water danced and played upon the shelving rock, as if to the laughing tune of the brook, and overhead weeping birches and hazels, and beside me green grass and wood hyacinths and primroses. All around the birds were singing with "full-throated ease," and up above, a deep blue sky with a few island clouds, and now and then, far up, a solitary crow winging across the blue and silence. Now this I call rest and peace. It is such an hour of rest amidst toil as does my soul good, lasts and will come back with a soothing peacefulness amidst hard labor.

I felt so thankful for my creation, my profession, my country, my all, all, all. I only desired something better in the spirit.

Pray don't smile at my burn; but when I feel in love, I delight to expatiate upon my beloved; and I am mad about my burn.

————

FRANCIS JEFFREY TO CHARLES WILKES.

CRAIGCROOK HOUSE, May 9, 1818.

I began my vacation by writing you a long letter, and I shall end it in the same virtuous manner, for we move into town to-morrow, and my labors begin the day after. We have had some idleness and tranquillity here, and about *seven* fine days, but it has been a sad season on the whole, first with cold and then with wet; and as I am laying down my twelve acres in grass, I have had my fair share of a young farmer's anxieties and mortifications. However, I bear all my trials manfully, and when I cannot be quite resigned I try to make a joke of them. Neither Charley nor I understand much about rain or dirt, and we are both so fond of woodlands and mountains that we have scarcely missed a day without trudging out, and climbing away among mists and showers and craggy places, with scarcely a primrose to cheer us, and nothing but the loneliness and freshness of the scene to put us in good humor. It has long been my opinion that those who have a genuine love for nature and rural scenery are very easily pleased, and that it is not easy to find any aspect of the sky or the earth from which they will not borrow delight. For my own part, condemned as I am to a great deal of town life, there is something delicious to me in the sound even of a biting east wind among my woods; and the sight of a clear spring bubbling from a rock, and the smell of the budding pines and the common field daisies, and the cawing of my rooks, and the cooing of my cushats, are almost enough for me—so at least I think to-day, which is a kind of parting day for them, and endears them all more than ever. Do not imagine, however, that we have nothing better, for we have now hyacinths, auriculas, and anemones, in great glory, besides sweetbrier, and wallflowers in abundance, and blue gentians and violets, and plenty of rose leaves, though no flowers yet, and apple-blossoms and sloes all around. . . .

————

FRANCIS JEFFREY TO MRS. JAMES CRAIG.

DUNKELD, Friday, September 20, 1839.

I thought I should have written to you from Rothiemurchus! Would not that have been nice? But I cannot get any nearer. . . . It is something, however, to have peeped even so far into the threshold of your central highlands, to have smelt the peat smoke of your cottages, heard the sweet chime of your rocky cascades, and seen your shiny cliffs starting from every birch and dark pine, and the blue ridges of your distant hills melting into the inland sky. I need

not tell *you* what recollections are awakened by
these objects, nor how fresh, at such moments,
all the visions of youth, and the deeper tinted,
and scarcely less glorious, dreams of manhood,
come back upon the heart. I have been thinking, all day, of one of the last, I rather think it
was *the* last time I saw you at Rothiemurchus,
and of a long rambling ride we had, upon
ponies, through the solemn twilight of a dark
autumnal day. The birches and oak copses
were all of a deep tawny yellow, the pines
spreading far over the plains of an inky blue, a
broad band of saffron light gleaming sadly in
the west, and the Spey sweeping and sounding
hoarsely below us, as we paused, for a long
time, on a height near the gamekeeper's house.
Have you any recollection of the same? I
remember it as if it were yesterday, or rather
feel it as if it were still before me. Why, or
how, I cannot tell. But there it is; as vivid,
and clear, and real, as when it was present to my
senses. And it is as real and true, if memory
and feeling be as much parts of our nature as
our senses, and give us the same assurance of
the existence of their objects. . . .

COMEDY AND FARCE.

MISS HANNAH MORE TO MRS. GWATKIN.

August 9, 1778.

. . . When your letter was brought, I was upon a visit in the neighborhood, where it was sent me. There were ten ladies and a clergyman. I was pleased with the assemblage, thinking the vanity of the *sex* would meet with its equilibrium in the wisdom of the *profession :* that the brilliant sallies of female wit and sprightliness would be corrected and moderated by the learned gravity and judicious conversation of the Rev. Theologue. I looked upon the latter as the centripetal, acting against the centrifugal force of the former, who would be kept within their orbit of decorum by his means. For about an hour nothing was uttered but *words*, which are almost an equivalent to nothing. The gentleman had not yet spoken. The *ladies*, with loud vociferation, seemed to *talk* much without *thinking* at all. The gentleman, with all the male stupidity of

116

silent recollection, without saying a single syllable, seemed to be acting over the pantomime
of thought. I cannot say indeed his countenance so much belied his understanding as to
express any thing: no, let me not do him that in-
justice ; he might have sat for the picture of insensibility. I endured his taciturnity, thinking
that the longer he was in collecting, adjusting
and arranging his ideas, the more would he
charm me with the tide of oratorical eloquence,
when the materials of his conversation were
ready for display : but, alas ! it never occurred
that I had seen an *empty* bottle corked as well
as a *full* one. After sitting another hour, I
thought I perceived in him signs of pregnant
sentiment, which was just on the point of being
delivered in speech. I was extremely exhila-
rated at this, but it was a false alarm : he es-
sayed it not ; at length the imprisoned powers
.of rhetoric burst through the shallow mounds
of torpid silence and reserve, and he remarked,
with equal acuteness of wit, novelty and invention, and depth of penetration, that " we had
had no summer." Then, shocked at his own
loquacity, he double-locked the door of his lips,
" *and word spoke never more.*" . . .

SIR WALTER SCOTT TO HIS DAUGHTER.

ABBOTSFORD, March 23, 1825.

I am afraid you will think me a merciless correspondent, assailing you with so close a fire of letters; but having a frank I thought it as well to send you an epistle, though it can contain nothing more of interest, excepting that we are all well. . . .

I had proceeded thus far in my valuable communication, when, lo! I was alarmed by the entrance of that terrific animal, a two-legged boar—one of the largest size and most tremendous powers.   By the way, I learned, from no less an authority than George Canning, what my own experience has since made good, that an efficient bore must always have something respectable about him, otherwise no one would permit him to exercise his occupation. He must be, for example, a very rich man (which perhaps gives the greatest privilege of all), or he must be a man of rank and condition too important to be treated *sans ceremonie*, or a man of learning (often a dreadful bore), or of talents undoubted, or of high pretensions to wisdom and experience, or a great traveller; in short, he must have some tangible

privilege to sanction his profession. Without
something of this kind one would treat a bore
as you do a vagrant mendicant, and send him
off to the workhouse if he presumed to annoy
you. But when properly qualified the bore is
more like a beggar with a badge and pass from
his parish, which entitles him to disturb you
with his importunity whether you will or no.
Now, my bore is a complete gentleman, and an
old friend, but, unhappily for those who know
him, master of all Joe Miller's stories of sailors
and Irishmen, and full of quotations from the
classics as hackneyed as the post-horses of
Melrose. There was no remedy; I must
either stand his shot within doors, or turn out
with him for a long walk, and for the sake of
elbow-room I preferred the last. Imagine an
old gentleman, who has been handsome, and
has still that sort of pretension which leads
him to wear tight pantaloons and a smart half-
boot, neatly adapted to show off his leg; suppose him as upright and straight as a poker, if
the poker's head had been by some accident
bent to one side; add to this that he is as deaf
as a post; consider that I was writing to Jane,
and desired not to be interrupted by much

more entertaining society. Well, I was *had*, however—fairly caught—and out we sallied to make the best we could of each other. I felt a sort of necessity to ask him to dinner, but the invitation, like Macbeth's *amen*, stuck in my throat. For the first hour he got the lead, and kept it; but opportunities always occur to an able general, if he knows how to make use of them. In an evil hour for him and a happy one for me, he started the topic of our intended railroad; *there* I was a match for him, having had, on Tuesday last, a meeting with Harden, the two Torwoodlees, and the engineer, on this subject, so that I had at my finger-end every *cut*, every lift, every degree of elevation or depression, every pass in the country, and every possible means of crossing them. So I kept the whip-hand of him completely, and never permitted him to get off the railway again to his own ground. In short, so thoroughly did I bore my bore that he sickened and gave in, taking a short leave of me. Seeing him in full retreat, I *then* ventured to make the civil offer of a dinner. But the railroad had been breakfast, luncheon, dinner, and supper to boot; he hastily excused himself, and left me at double-

quick time, sick of railroads, I dare say, for six
months to come.   But I must not forget that
I am perhaps abusing the privilege I have to
bore you, being that of your affectionate
papa. . . .

SIR DAVID WILKIE TO MISS WILKIE.

JERUSALEM, March 31, 1841.

. . . We have been to the synagogues of
Mount Zion, where the women are present as
listeners, and where they read parts of the
books of Moses.   I went to a Saturday morning service, in a small out-house of a private
dwelling.   I went through snow, hail, and rain
to a crowded assembly, where I found them
chanting from the book of Numbers, of the
wrath of Moses at the golden calf. . . .

Such is the disposition for traffic among the
Jews that whilst I was witnessing this, to me,
impressive scene, the Turkish cavash of the
Consul brought from the bazaar a Damascus
cloak for me to purchase.   When the Rabbi
saw it he was in the act of reading the psalm,
"If I forget thee, O Jerusalem, let my right
hand forget her cunning."   King David gave
way to the Damascus cloak, and he instantly
exclaimed before all the people that the price

the merchant had agreed to take was thirteen dollars, and that the cloak was cheap at that money.   It was with difficulty that I could get away from him without striking the bargain or producing a commotion in the assembly.   The cloak I got afterwards for eleven dollars. . . .

RICHARD HARRIS BARHAM TO MRS. HUGHES.

CLIFTON, May 27, 1845.

. . . And now as to our state here—it is mended, and I would fain hope mending, but very, very slowly.   I am still not allowed—nor if I were could I avail myself of the permission —to answer, except in a whisper, and that only to ask for what I want, and answer medical enquiries.   Luckily I have assigned to me one of the greatest chatterboxes of a surgeon, to take the poking and blistering department of my treatment upon him, that can well be im- agined.   If in the multitude of counsellors there be wisdom, in that of apothecaries there is jaw, and with such a one as my adviser pos- sesses, Samson might have laid waste all Meso- potamia, let alone Philistia.   He has the art of saying nothing in a cascade of language com- parable only to that " almighty water privilege,"

Niagara, and were I in better spirits would delight instead of boring me. Galt's "weariful
woman" was but a type of him.

"Well, sir, how are we to-day—better, eh!
well, sir, go on with the iodine? does it act?"

"Why, that is what I wanted to ask; how do
you mean it to act? as a sudorific?"

"Diaphoretic we say, but sudorific will do;
it comes from *sudo*, but we seldom now say
sudorific; but, sir, the iodine, does it act?"

"That is just what I want to know; how do
you mean it to act, on the throat, or ——"

"Act? iodine? on the throat? why the
throat, sir, is very singulary constructed—very
singularly; it's beautiful the mechanism of the
throat! and if it gets out of order—now yours,
sir, is out of order, and we have been giving
you iodine—for Mr. —— agrees with me that
iodine is an excellent medicine, and what I
want to know is, does it begin to produce any
effect?"

"Why that is what I want to know, and
therefore I ask what effect is it intended to
produce; is it to act on —— "

"What effect? my dear sir, there are few
medicines now in better repute than iodine;

we give it in many cases—dropsy, sometimes
—not that yours is dropsy; you have nothing
dropsical about you; your complaint is an
affection of the throat, and we have been giving you iodine in your case—you have had it
now for three days—twice a day. Do you
take it regularly twice a day?"

"I take what you send me twice a day, and
you tell me it is iodine, but —— "

"And does it begin to produce its effect;
does it act?"

"Why that's what I'm asking you; now is
it intended to act as a sedative, or —— "

"A sedative? what, is your cough more
troublesome? We give sedatives sometimes for
troublesome coughs, and then in nervous com-
plaints, but then congestion is a thing to be
avoided, not that I see any symptoms of congestion in your case; yours is an affection of
the throat, and so we give you iodine, and as
we are a little particular in proportioning our
doses, I want to ascertain whether what you
have been taking acts?"

O dear, O dear! never were two philosophers
more deeply engaged in pursuing the same en-
quiry, each endeavoring to extract information

out of the other. And then such lectures on the
"anatomy of the parts," "the beautiful mechanism," etc.! that I, who never could compre-
hend the mechanism of a mouse-trap, and
hardly that of a poacher's wire, am just in the
position of a blind man listening to a discourse
on colors, and yet in the end completely worked
up into a something derived from *sudo*. Heaven
knows that I am at this moment as innocent of
any knowledge of the mode of operation of
" iodine " as a " blassed babe," though taking
" two tablespoonfuls a day " with this tea-
spoonful of learning. . . .

MISS MARY RUSSELL MITFORD TO SIR WILLIAM
ELFORD.

BERTRAM HOUSE, January 9, 1819.

Considering my doleful prognostications,
you will like to know, my dear friend, that I
have outlived the ball, so I must write. It 's a
thing of necessity. Yes, I am living and "life-
lich," as Chaucer says. And that I did survive
that dreaded night I owe principally to that
charming thing—a dandy. Don't you like
dandies, the beautiful race? I am sure you
must. But such a dandy as our dandy few

have been fortunate enough to see. In general
they are on a small scale—slim, whipper-snap-
per youths, fresh from college—or new mounted
on a dragoon's saddle—dainty light horsemen,
or trim schoolboys. Ours is of a Patagonian
breed—six feet and upwards without his shoes,
and broad in proportion. Unless you have
seen a wasp in a solar microscope, you have
never seen any thing like him. Perhaps a
Brobdignagian hour-glass might be more like
him still, only I don't think the hour-glass
would be small enough in the waist.

Great as my admiration has always been of
the mechanical inventions of this age, I know
nothing that has given me so high an idea of
the power of machinery—not the Portsmouth
Block-houses, or the new Mint—as that perfection of mechanism by which those ribs are
endued in those stays. I think one or two
must have been broken, to render such a com-
pression possible. But it is unjust to dwell so
exclusively on the stays, when every part of
the thing was equally perfect. Trowsers—
coat—neckcloth—shirt-collar—head, inside and
out—all were in exact keeping. Every look,
every word, every attitude belonged to those

inimitable stays. Sweet dandy! I have seen nothing like him since Liston, in "Lord Grizzle." He kept me awake and alive the whole evening. Dancing or sitting still, he was my "cynosure." I followed him with my eyes as a schoolboy follows the vagaries of his top or the rolling of his hoop. Much and generally as he was admired, I don't think he made so strong an impression on any one as on me. He is even indebted to me for the distinguished attention of a great wit, whose shafts I was lucky enough to direct to that impenetrable target of dandyism. All this he owes to me, and is likely to owe me still, for I am sorry to say my dandy is an ungrateful dandy. Our admiration was by no means mutual. "He had an idea," he said (a very bold assertion, by-the-by)—"he had an idea that I was bluish." So he scoured away on being threatened with an introduction. Well, peace be to him, poor swain! and better fortune—for the poor dandy is rather unlucky. He fell into the Thames last summer on a water-party and got wet through his stays; and this autumn, having affronted a young lady, and being knocked down by her brother, a lad not nineteen, he had the misfortune to fall flat

on his back, and was forced to lie till some one
came to pick him up, being too straight-laced
to help himself. . . .

WILLIAM COWPER TO JOHN NEWTON.

OLNEY, March 29, 1784.

It being his majesty's pleasure that I should
yet have another opportunity to write before
he dissolves the parliament, I avail myself of it
with all possible alacrity. I thank you for your
last, which was not the less welcome for coming,
like an extraordinary gazette, at a time when
it was not expected.

As when the sea is uncommonly agitated,
the water finds its way into creeks and holes of
rocks, which in its calmer state it never reaches,
in like manner the effect of these turbulent
times is felt even at Orchard Side, where in
general we live as undisturbed by the political
element, as shrimps or cockles that have been
accidentally deposited in some hollow beyond
the water-mark, by the unusual dashing of the
waves. We were sitting yesterday after dinner,
the two ladies and myself, very composedly,
and without the least apprehension of any such
intrusion in our snug parlor, one lady knitting,
the other netting, and the gentleman winding

worsted, when to our unspeakable surprise a
mob appeared before the window; a smart rap
was heard at the door, the boys halloo'd, and
the maid announced Mr. Grenville. Puss was
unfortunately let out of her box, so that the
candidate, with all his good friends at his heels,
was refused admittance at the grand entry, and
referred to the back door, as the only possible
way of approach.

Candidates are creatures not very susceptible
of affronts, and would rather, I suppose, climb
in at a window than be absolutely excluded. In
a minute, the yard, the kitchen, and the parlor
were filled. Mr. Grenville advancing toward
me shook me by the hand with a degree of
cordiality that was extremely seducing. As
soon as he and as many more as could find
chairs were seated, he began to open the intent
of his visit. I told him I had no vote, for
which he readily gave me credit. I assured
him I had no influence, which he was not
equally inclined to believe, and the less, no
doubt, because Mr. Ashburner, the draper, ad-
dressing himself to me at this moment, informed me that I had a great deal. Supposing
that I could not be possessed of such a treasure

without knowing it, I ventured to confirm my
first assertion, by saying that if I had any I
was utterly at a loss to imagine where it could
be, or wherein it consisted. Thus ended the
conference. Mr. Grenville squeezed me by the
hand again, kissed the ladies, and withdrew.
He kissed likewise the maid in the kitchen, and
seemed upon the whole a most loving, kissing,
kind-hearted gentleman. He is very young,
genteel, and handsome. He has a pair of very
good eyes in his head, which not being sufficient as it should seem for the many nice and
difficult purposes of the senator, he has a third
also, which he wore suspended by a riband
from his buttonhole. The boys halloo'd, the
dogs barked, Puss scampered ; the hero, with
his long train of obsequious followers, withdrew. We made ourselves very merry with
the adventure, and in a short time settled into
our former tranquillity, never probably to be
thus interrupted more. I thought myself, however, happy in being able to affirm truly that I
had not the influence for which he sued ; and
which, had I been possessed of it, with my
present views of the dispute between the Crown
and the Commons, I must have refused him,

for he is on the side of the former. It is comfortable to be of no consequence in a world where one cannot exercise any without disobliging somebody. The town however seems to be much at his service, and if he be equally successful throughout the country, he will undoubtedly gain his election. Mr. Ashburner perhaps was a little mortified because it was evident that I owed the honor of this visit to his misrepresentation of my importance. But had he thought proper to assure Mr. Grenville that I had three heads, I should not I suppose have been bound to produce them. . . .

BENJAMIN ROBERT HAYDON TO MISS MARY RUSSELL MITFORD.

August 18, 1826.

How do you find yourself? I heard you were poorly. What are you about? I was happy to hear of ——'s safe arrival again, and I shall be most happy to see him, though tell him he will find no more " Solomons " towering up as a background to our conversations. Nothing but genteel-sized drawing-room pocket-history—Alexander in a nutshell ; Bucephalus no bigger than a Shetland pony, and my little girl's doll a giantess to my Olympias.

The other night I paid my butcher; one of the miracles of these times, you will say. Let me tell you I have all my life been seeking for a butcher whose respect for genius predominated over his love of gain. I could not make out, before I dealt with this man, his excessive desire that I should be his customer; his sly hints as I passed his shop that he had "a bit of South Down, very fine; a sweetbread, perfection; and a calf's foot that was all jelly without bone!" The other day he called, and I had him sent up into the painting-room. I found him in great admiration of "Alexander." "Quite alive, sir!" "I am glad you think so," said I. "Yes, sir, but, as I have said often to my sister, you could not have painted that picture, sir, if you had not eat my meat, sir!" "Very true, Mr. Sowerby." "Ah! sir, I have a fancy for *genus*, sir!" "Have you, Mr. Sowerby?" "Yes, sir; Mrs. Siddons, sir, has eat my meat, sir; never was *such a woman for chops*, sir!"—and he drew up his beefy, shiny face, clean shaved, with a clean blue cravat under his chin, a clean jacket, a clean apron, and a pair of hands that would pin an ox to the earth if he was obstreperous—"Ah! sir, she was a wonderful crayture!" "She was, Mr. Sowerby." "Ah, sir, when she used to act that there character, you see (but Lord, such a head! as I say to my sister)—that there woman, sir, that murders a king between 'm!" "Oh! Lady Macbeth." "Ah, sir, that 's it—Lady Macbeth—I used to get up with the butler behind her carriage when she acted, and, as I used to see her looking quite wild, and all the people quite frightened, Ah, ha! my lady, says I, if it was n't for my meat, though, you would n't be able to do *that!*" "Mr. Sowerby, you seem to be a man of feeling. Will you take a glass of wine?" After a bow or two, down he sat, and by degrees his heart opened. "You see, sir, I have fed Mrs. Siddons, sir; John Kemble, sir; Charles Kemble, sir; Stephen Kemble, sir; and Madame Catalani, sir; Morland the painter, and, I beg your pardon, sir, and *you*, sir." "Mr. Sowerby, you do me honor." "Madame Catalani, sir, was a wonderful woman for sweetbreads; but the Kemble family, sir, the gentlemen, sir, rump-steaks and kidneys in general was their taste; but Mrs. Siddons, sir, she liked chops, sir, as much as you do, sir," etc., etc. I soon perceived that the man's ambition was to feed genius. I shall recommend you to him; but is he not a capital fellow? but a little acting with his remarks would make you roar with laughter. Think of Lady Macbeth eating chops! Is this not a peep behind the curtain? . . .

MISS MARY RUSSELL MITFORD TO SIR WILLIAM ELFORD.

THREE-MILE CROSS, February 8, 1821.

. . . Mrs. Dickinson has had great success in match-making lately—an amusement of which, deny it as she may, she is remarkably fond. We have a celebrated beauty hereabouts, a Miss B——, a fine, gentleman-like, dashing, spirited girl, who, with the usual fate of beauties, attracted a good deal of admiration and very little love. On the other hand, there was a soft, lady-like, fair, delicate youth, with red whiskers and a great talent for silence, a great-grandson of three generations of Generals H——, who, well-born, well-bred, and well-estated, seemed just made to lean upon such a fine, manly supporter as Bessy B——. So thought Mrs. Dickinson, and the match is made; they are already deep in settlements and wedding-clothes—and the marriage will take place forthwith. How she brought him to the offer I cannot imagine. She says he did it all himself; but I don't believe her.

I must tell you of a misfortune that befell me in this case. I was dining at Farley Hill on the very day that it happened to strike Mrs. Dickinson that they would make a nice couple, and had the ill-luck to sit next to Mr. H—— at table ; he held his tongue in the most pro- voking manner possible, and, when I made him talk, talked, not nonsense, but the dullest, gravest, prosiest sense—vapid, stale, common- place—a hundred years behind the spirit of the age—such tame moralities as the first Gen- eral H—— might have discussed with one of Queen Anne's maids of honor.

Well, after dinner, as I was standing wearily before the drawing-room fire, indulging in the *ennui* engendered by Mr. H——'s silence and conversation, Mrs. Dickinson, full of her new project, and wanting my assistance to accom- plish it, brought Miss B—— up to me, and asked, in her quiet manner, " How do you like Mr. H——'s face? What does it express?" " Nothing," said I, in a lazy, truth-telling tone,

little dreaming that I was giving this flatter-
ing opinion before his future lady and love.

Notwithstanding this awkward blunder, I am
really glad of the match. They are both very
worthy and well-meaning young people—
though it 's a pity they can't change sexes ;
and there 's great chance of their improving
one another, and greater still of their being
happy together.

_____

WILLIAM COWPER TO JOHN NEWTON.

OLNEY, November 17, 1783.

. . . Since our conflagration here, we have
sent two women and one boy to the justice,
for depredation. . . . The young gentleman
who accompanied these fair ones, is the junior
son of Molly Boswell. He had stolen some
ironwork, the property of Griggs, the butcher.
Being convicted, he was ordered to be whipt,
which operation he underwent at the cart's tail,
from the stone-house to the high arch, and back
again. He seemed to show great fortitude,
but it was all an imposition upon the public.
The beadle, who performed, had filled his left
hand with red ochre, through which, after every
stroke, he drew the lash of his whip, leaving
the appearance of a wound upon the skin, but,
in reality, not hurting him at all. This being

perceived by Mr. Constable Hinschcomb, who
followed the beadle, he applied his cane, without any such management or precaution, to the
shoulders of the too merciful executioner. The
scene immediately became more interesting.
The beadle could by no means be prevailed
upon to strike hard, which provoked the constable to still harder ; and this double flogging
continued, till a lass of Silver-end, pitying the
pitiful beadle thus suffering under the hands of
the pitiless constable, joined the procession,
and, placing herself immediately behind the
latter, seized him by his capillary club, and,
pulling him backwards by the same, slapt his
face with a most Amazonian fury. This concat-
enation of events has taken up more of my
paper than I intended it should, but I could
not forbear to inform you how the beadle
threshed the thief, the constable the beadle,
and the lady the constable, and how the thief
was the only person concerned who suffered
nothing. . . .

CHARLES DICKENS TO MISS HOGARTH.

ROME, Sunday night, November 13, 1853.

. . . One night, at Naples, Edward came in,
open-mouthed, to the *table-d'hôte* where we
were dining with the Tennents, to announce

"The Marchese Garofalo." I at first thought it must be the little parrot-marquess who was once your escort from Genoa; but I found him to be a man (married to an Englishwoman) whom we used to meet at Ridgway's. He was very glad to see me, and I afterwards met him at dinner at Mr. Lowther's, our *chargé d'affaires.* Mr. Lowther was at the Rockingham play, and is a very agreeable fellow. We had an exceedingly pleasant dinner of eight, preparatory to which I was near having the ridiculous adventure of not being able to find the house and coming back dinnerless. I went in an open carriage from the hotel, in all state, and the coachman, to my surprise, pulled up at the end of the Chiaja. "Behold the house," says he, "of Il Signor Larthoor!" —at the same time pointing with his whip into the seventh heaven, where the early stars were shining. "But the Signor Larthoor," returns the inimitable darling, "lives at Pausilippo." "It is true," says the coachman (still pointing to the evening star), "but he lives high up the Salita Sant' Antonio, where no carriage ever yet ascended, and that is the house" (evening star, as aforesaid), "and one must go on foot.

Behold the Salita Sant' Antonio!" I went up
it, a mile and a half I should think. I got into
the strangest places, among the wildest Ne-
apolitans—kitchens, washing-places, archways,
stables, vineyards—was baited by dogs, answered in profoundly unintelligible Neapolitan,
from behind lonely, locked doors, in cracked female voices, quaking with fear ; could hear of no
such Englishman, or any Englishman. By-and-
by I came upon a Polenta-shop in the clouds,
where an old Frenchman, with an umbrella like
a faded tropical leaf (it had not rained for six
weeks) was staring at nothing at all, with a
snuff-box in his hand. To him I appealed concerning the Signor Larthoor. " Sir," said he,
with the sweetest politeness, " you can speak
French?" " Sir," said I, " a little." " Sir,"
said he, " I presume the Signor Loothere "—
you will observe that he changed the name according to the custom of his country—" is an
Englishman ?" I admitted that he was the
victim of circumstances and had that misfortune. " Sir," said he, " one word more. *Has*
he a servant with a wooden leg ?" " Great
heaven, sir," said I, " how do I know! I
should think not, but it is possible." " It is

always," said the Frenchman, "possible. Almost all the things of the world are always
possible." "Sir," said I,—you may imagine
my condition and dismal sense of my own
absurdity, by this time,—"that is true." He
then took an immense pinch of snuff, wiped
the dust off his umbrella, led me to an arch
commanding a wonderful view of the Bay of
Naples, and pointed deep into the earth from
which I had mounted. "Below there, near the
lamp, one finds an Englishman, with a servant
with a wooden leg. It is always possible that
he is the Signor Loothere." I had been asked
at six, and it was now getting on for seven.
I went down again in a state of perspiration
and misery not to be described, and without
the faintest hope of finding the place. But
as I was going down to the lamp, I saw the
strangest staircase up a dark corner, with a
man in a white waistcoat (evidently hired)
standing on the top of it, fuming. I dashed
in at a venture, found it was the place, made
the most of the whole story, and was inde-
scribably popular. The best of it was, that
as nobody ever did find the place, he had put
a servant at the bottom of the Salita, to

"wait for an English gentleman." The servant (as he presently pleaded), deceived by the
moustache, had allowed the English gentleman
to pass unchallenged. . . .

MISS ELIZABETH CARTER TO MISS CATHERINE
TALBOT.

CANTERBURY, April 15, 1749.

I got safe to this place on Thursday night,
after as pleasant a journey as could happen to
anybody who hates every coach in the world but
one. As the common stage was full, we set
out in a creditable-looking landau, and only four
passengers, consisting of two of the quietest,
gentlest Frenchwomen I ever met with, and
one who seemed to be a good kind of an English body, but somewhat apprehensive of *ac-
cidences ;* and a very untoward accidence was
certainly our fate, for while we were rejoicing at
the easiness of our conveyance, and greatly disposed to be pleased with each other, 't is not to
be imagined the supreme consternation that appeared in all our faces, when at the end of two
miles we beheld the fattest and most magnificent of all gentlewomen, who, with a most
boisterous air, demanded admittance, which nobody seemed willing to grant her; but, how-

ever, in a most violent passion she forced her
way, and in an instant occupied three quarters
of the coach. The poor Françoises appeared
absolutely overcome, and without resistance
were drove into the smallest of all corners, with
great meekness observing, "*Assurément cette
femme agit très cavaliérement.*" For my own
part, I could not help wishing for Lucian's
Menippus, to divest the good woman of her
superfluities ; for if he had stripped her of the
pompous gold brocade, and the bed-gown over
that, and the velvet cloak that covered the bed-
gown, she might have been reduced to the
moderate size of any two or three gentlewomen
of these degenerate days, and her fellow-travel-
lers been greatly relieved. However, I was
obliged to her for more diversion than I expected, and laughed very heartily all the way,
which to be sure was very rude ; but there was
no fear of abashing her, for on observing the
miserable wry faces of most of the company,
she declared that let folks look, or say what
they would, it was always her rule to be at her
ease, which accordingly she most strictly
observed, and for about thirty miles squeezed
poor suffering people to death with the most
perfect composure to herself. . . .

CHELSEA, July 16, 1858.

. . . I could swear you never heard of Madame —— de ——. But she has heard of you; and if you were in the habit of thanking God "for the blessing made to fly over your head," you might offer a modest thanksgiving for the honor that stunning lady did you in galloping madly all around Hyde Park in chase of your "brown wide-awake" the last day you rode there; no mortal could predict what the result would be if she came up with you. To seize your bridle and look at you till she was satisfied was a trifle to what she was supposed capable of. She only took to galloping after you when more legitimate means had failed.

She circulates everywhere, this madcap "Frenchwoman." She met "the Rev. John" (Barlow), and said, when he was offering delicate attentions, "There is just one thing I wish you would do for me—to take me to see Mr. Carlyle." "Tell me to ask the Archbishop of Canterbury to dance a polka with you," said Barlow, aghast, "and I would dare it, though I have not the honor of his acquaintance; but take anybody to Mr. Carlyle—impossible!"

" That silly old Barlow won't take me to
Carlyle," said the lady to George Cook; " you
must do it then." "Gracious heavens!" said
George Cook; " ask me to take you up to the
Queen, and introduce you to her, and I would
do it, and 'take the six months' imprisonment,'
or whatever punishment was awarded me; but
take anybody to Mr. Carlyle—impossible!"

Soon after this, George Cook met her riding
in the Park, and said: " I passed Mr. Carlyle a
little way on, in his brown wide-awake." The
lady lashed her horse and set off in pursuit,
leaving her party out of sight, and went all
round the Park at full gallop, looking out for
the wide-awake. . . .

———

THOMAS CHALMERS TO ——

EDINBURGH, October 5, 1824.

. . . You would be amused with the state of
matters here, Miss —— evidently making a
great effort both to accommodate me and to
abstain from pressing. She makes open pro-
clamation of my freedom, protests that she will
make no infringement thereupon—is determined to act up strictly to the principle of leaving me to myself; and if she would simply and

silently do so, it were most delightful. But she is very loud in the profession of this her own system, and withal so very fearful, and so obviously so of even the slightest encroachment upon it, that while she studies to abstain from all restraints upon me, she gives me a feeling that I am a very great restraint upon her. She is a truly kind and pleasant person notwithstanding, though her treatment is calculated to give a bystander the impression that I am a very sensitive and singular person withal. She never asks the same thing twice of me, but she makes up for this by the exceeding multitude of these things, such as, if my tea is right—if I would like more sugar—if I take cream—if I am fond of little or much cream—if I would take butter to my cake——when I take to loaf, if I take butter to my white bread—if I move from one part of the room to another, whether I would like to sit on the sofa—after I have sat there, whether I would like to stretch out my legs upon it—after I have done that, whether I would let her wheel it nearer the fire—when I move to my bed-room, whether the fire is right —whether I would like the blinds wound up? etc., etc. She at the same time most religiously abstains from repetitions, but to reply even once to her indefinite number of proposals is fatigue enough, I can assure you ; nor is the fatigue at all alleviated, when, instead of coming forth a second time with each, she comes forth with a most vehement asseveration, accompanied by uplifted hands, that she will let me do as I like, that she will not interfere, that I shall have liberty in her house ; and when I said that it behooved me to make calls immediately after dinner, she declared that I would have leave to go away with my dinner in my mouth if I chose. I have got the better of all this by downright laughing, for I verily think now that the case is altogether desperate.

THOMAS HOOD TO CHARLES WENTWORTH DILKE.

COBLENZ, May 6, 1835.

. . . Our servant knows a few words of English, too; her name is *Gradle,* the short for Margaret. Jane wanted a fowl to boil for me. Now she has a theory that the more she makes her English un-English, the more it must be like German. Jane begins by showing Gradle a word in the dictionary.

Gradle.—"Ja! yees — hühn — henne — ja! yees."

Jane (a little through her nose).—" Hmn—
hum—hem—yes—yaw, ken you geet a fowl—
fool—foal, to boil—bile—bole for dinner?"

Gradle.—" Hot wasser?"

Jane.—"Yaw, in pit—pat—pot—hmn—hum
—eh!"

Gradle (a little off the scent again).—" Ja,
nein—wasser, pot—hot—nein."

Jane.—"Yes—no—good to eeat—chicken—
cheeken — checking — choking — bird—bard —
beard—lays eggs—eeggs—hune, heine—hin—
make cheekin broth—soup—poultry—peltry—
paltry!"

Gradle (quite at fault).—" Pfeltrighchtch!—
nein."

Jane (in despair).—"What shall I do! and
Hood won't help me, he only laughs. This
comes of leaving England!" (She casts her
eyes across the street at the governor's poultry-
yard, and a bright thought strikes her.) " Here,
Gradle—come here—comb hair—hmn—hum—
look there—dare—you see things walking—
hmn, hum, wacking about—things with feathers—fathers—feethers."

Gradle (hitting it off again).—" Feethers—fa-
ders—ah hah! fedders—ja, ja, yees, sie bringen
—fedders, ja, ja!"

Jane echoes " Fedders—yes—yaw, yaw ! "

Exit Gradle, and after three-quarters of an hour, returns triumphantly with two bundles of stationer's quills !!! . . .

BENJAMIN ROBERT HAYDON TO MARY RUSSELL MITFORD.

March 28, 1825.

. . . I was at Soane's * last night to see this sarcophagus by lamp-light. The first person I met, after seventeen years, was Coleridge; silver-haired, he looked at my bald front, and I at his hair, with mutual looks of sympathy, and mutual head-shaking. It affected me very much, and so it seemed to affect him. I did not know what to say, nor did he ; and then, in his chanting way, half-poetical, half-inspired, half-idiotic, he began to console me by trying to prove that the only way for a man of genius to be happy was just to put forth no more power than was sufficient for the purposes of the age in which he lived, as if genius was a power one could fold up like a parasol ! At this moment over came Spurzheim, with his

* Sir John Soane, architect and R. A. His house, described in this letter, is now the Soane Museum, Lincoln's Inn Fields.

German simplicity, and shaking my hand: "How doe you doe? Vy, your organs are more parfaite den eaver. How luckee you lose your hair. Veel you pearmeet me to introwdooze you to Mrs. Spurzheim?" I was pushed against Turner, the landscape painter, with his red face and white waistcoat, and before I could see Mrs. Spurzheim, was carried off my legs, and irretrievably bustled to where the sarcophagus lay.

Soane's house is a perfect Cretan labyrinth: curious narrow staircases, landing-places, balconies, spring doors, and little rooms filled with fragments to the very ceiling. It was the finest fun imaginable to see the people come into the library after wandering about below, amidst tombs and capitals, and shafts, and noseless heads, with a sort of expression of delighted relief at finding themselves again among the living, and with coffee and cake! They looked as if they were pleased to feel their blood circulate once more, and went smirking up to Soane, " lui faisant leurs compliments," with a twisting chuckle of features as if grateful for their escape. Fancy delicate ladies of fashion dipping their pretty heads into an old, mouldy, fusty, hieroglyphicked coffin, blessing their stars at its age, wondering whom it contained, and whispering that it was mentioned in Pliny. You can imagine the associations connected with such contrasts. Just as I was beginning to meditate, the Duke of Sussex, with a star on his breast, and an asthma inside it, came squeezing and wheezing along the narrow passage, driving all the women before him like a Bluebeard, and, putting his royal head in the coffin, added his wonder to the wonder of the rest. Upstairs stood Soane, spare, thin, caustic, and starched, "mocking the thing he laughed at," as he smiled approbation for the praises bestowed on his magnificent house. . . . Coleridge said: "I have a great contempt for these Egyptians with all their learning. After all, what did it amount to, but a bad system of astronomy?" "What do *you* think of this house, Mr. Haydon?" said that dandy, ——, to me. "Very interesting," I said. "Very interesting," he replied, with a sparkle in his eye denoting an occult meaning he was too polite to express. "Very curious, is it not?" "Very curious," I echoed. "Very kind of Mr. Soane to open the house so." "Very kind," I replied, as grave as the Chan-

cellor, seeing that he was dying to say something which would come out if I pretended ig-
norance. " Rather odd, though, stuck about
so." I smiled. " However, it *is* very kind of
Soane, you know, but it 's a funny house, and
a——" Just then, Soane was elbowed against
him, and both making elegant bows to the
other, —— expressed his thanks to Soane for
"admitting him to the enjoyment of such a
splendid treat," etc., etc.,—and he went off
with Soane downstairs, talking of the Egyptians
with all the solemnity of deep learning and of
a profound interest in his subject.

As I looked at Soane, smiling and flushed by
flattery, I thought of Johnson at Ranelagh.
" There was not a soul then around him who
would not, ere they put on their night-caps,
envy him his assemblage of rank, and talent,
and fashion ; sneer at his antiques, quiz his
coffee, and go to sleep, pitying with affected
superiority his delusion and vanity." But
Soane is a good, though caustic man. .   .
And now I must go and paint the carpet my
sitter stands on ; so adieu to human nature,
and let me paint with all my power the color
and the texture of a Brussels bit. . . .

CHARLES LAMB TO SAMUEL TAYLOR COLERIDGE.

October 9, 1800.

I suppose you have heard of the death of Amos
Cottle.   I paid a solemn visit of condolence to
his brother, accompanied by George Dyer, of
burlesque memory.   I went, trembling to see
poor Cottle so immediately upon the event. He
was in black, and his younger brother was also
in black.   Every thing wore an aspect suitable
to the respect due to the freshly dead.   For
some time after our entrance, nobody spake till
George modestly put in a question, whether
" Alfred " was likely to sell.   This was Lethe
to Cottle,* and his poor face, wet with tears,
and his kind eye brightened up in a moment.
Now I felt it was my cue to speak.   I had to
thank him for a present of a magnificent copy,
and had promised to send him my remarks—
the least thing I could do ; so I ventured to
suggest that I perceived a considerable improvement he had made in his first book since
the state in which he first read it to me. Joseph,
who till now had sat with his knees cowering in
by the fire-place, wheeled about, and with great

* Joseph Cottle, the surviving brother, had recently published " Alfred, an Epic Poem."

difficulty of body shifted the same round to the corner of a table where I was sitting, and first stationing one thigh over the other, which is his sedentary mood, and placidly fixing his benevolent face right against mine, waited my observations. At that moment it came strongly into my mind, that I had got Uncle Toby before me, he looked so kind and so good. I could not say an unkind thing of "Alfred." So I set my memory to work to recollect what was the name of Alfred's queen, and with some adroitness recalled the well-known sound to Cottle's ears of Alswitha. At that moment I could perceive that Cottle had forgot his brother was so lately become a blessed spirit. In the language of mathematicians the author was as 9, the brother as 1. I felt my cue, and strong pity working at the root, I went to work and beslabbered "Alfred" with most unqualified praise, or only qualifying my praise, by the occasional politic interposition of an exception taken against trivial faults, slips, and human imperfections, which, by removing the appearance of insincerity, did but in truth heighten the relish. Perhaps I might have spared that refinement, for Joseph was in a humor to hope and believe

all things. What I said was beautifully supported, corroborated, and confirmed by the
stupidity of his brother on my left hand, and
by George on my right, who has an utter inca-
pacity for comprehending that there can be
any thing bad in poetry. All poems are *good*
poems to George; all men are *fine geniuses.* So
what with my actual memory, of which I made
the most, and Cottle's own helping me out, for
I *really* had forgotten a good deal of " Alfred," I
made shift to discuss the most essential parts
entirely to the satisfaction of its author, who
repeatedly declared that he loved nothing better than *candid* criticism. Was I a candid grey-
hound now for all this? or did I do right? I
believe I did. The effect was luscious to my
conscience. For all the rest of the evening
Amos was no more heard of, till George revived
the subject by inquiring whether some account
should not be drawn up by some of the friends
of the deceased, to be inserted in Phillips's
Monthly Obituary; adding that Amos was
estimable both for his head and heart, and
would have made a fine poet if he had lived.
To the expediency of this measure Cottle fully
assented, but could not help adding that he

always thought that the qualities of his brother's heart exceeded those of his head. I believe
his brother, when living, had formed precisely
the same idea of him; and I apprehend the
world will assent to both judgments. I rather
guess that the brothers were poetical rivals. I
judged so when I saw them together. Poor
Cottle, I must leave him, after his short dream,
to muse again upon his poor brother, for whom
I am sure in secret he will yet shed many a
tear. . . .

MISS SYDNEY OWENSON (AFTERWARDS LADY MOR-
GAN) TO HER FATHER.

ST. ANDREW'S STREET, DUBLIN, 1796 (?) *

You see how soon I begin to fulfil your com-
mands, for you are not many hours gone. But
you bid me not let a day pass before I began
a journal and telling you all that happens to
your two poor loving little girls, who never
were so unhappy in all their lives as when they
saw the yellow chaise wheels turn down the
corner of Trinity Street, and lost sight of you.
There we remained with our necks stretched

* Making allowance for the varying statements concerning
Lady Morgan's age, this letter must have been written when
she was between thirteen and fifteen years old.

out of the window, and Molly crying over us:
" Musha, Musha !" when looking up, she suddenly cried out : " See what God has sent to
comfort ye !" and it was indeed remarkable that
at that very moment the heavy clouds that rested
over the dome of the round church just opposite,
broke away, and in a burst of sunshine down
came flying a beautiful gold-colored bird, very
much resembling that beautiful picture in the
picture-gallery in Kilkenny Castle, which we
so lately saw.   Well, sir, it came fluttering down
to the very sill of the window, Molly thinking,
I believe, it was a miracle sent to comfort us,
when, lo and behold, dear papa, what should it
turn out to be but Mrs. Stree's old Tom pigeon,
who roosts every night on the top of St. Andrew's, and whom her mischievous son *had
painted yellow !*

Olivia made great game of Saint Molly and
her miracle, and made such a funny sketch of
her as made me die laughing, and that cheered
us both up.   After breakfast, Molly dressed us
" neat as hands and pins could make us," she
said, and we went to church ; but just as we
were stepping out of the hall door, who should
come plump against us but James Carter, and

he looked so well and handsome in his new college robe and square cap (the first time he had
ever put them on), and a beautiful prayer-book
in his hand, that we really did not know him.
He said he had forgotten to leave a message
for us on his way to the college chapel, from
his grandma, to beg that we would come in
next door and dine with her, as we must be
very lonely after our father's departure, which
offer, of course, we accepted ; and he said with
his droll air : " If you will allow me the honor,
I will come in and escort you at four o'clock."
" No, sir," said Molly, who hates him, and who
said he only wanted to come in and have a
romp with Miss Livy, "there is no need, as
your grandmamma lives only next door" ; and
so we went to church and Molly went to Mass ;
and all this diverted our grief, though it did not
vanquish it. Well, we had such a nice dinner !
It is impossible to tell you how droll James
Carter was, and how angry he made the dear
old lady, who put him down constantly, with,
" You forget, sir, that you are now a member
of the most learned university in the world,
and no longer a scrubby school-boy." Well,
the cloth was scarcely removed and grace said

by James (by-the-by with such a long face),
when he started up and said : "Come, girls,
let us have a stroll in the College Park whilst
granny takes her nap." Oh, if you could only
see granny's face. "*No*, sir," said she, "the
girls, as you are pleased to call the young
ladies, your cousins, shall *not* go and stroll with
you among a pack of young collegians and
audacious nursery-maids. Now that you are a
member of the most learned university in the
world, you might stay quiet at home on the
Lord's day, and read a sermon for your young
friends, or at least recommend them some good
book to read 'whilst granny takes her nap.'"
All this time Jem looked the image of Maw-
worm in the play, and then taking two books
off the window-seats, he gave one to each of
us, and said : "Mark, learn, and inwardly
*di*gest till I return." The next moment he was
flying by the window and kissing hands, and so
granny and the old black cat purring together
fell fast asleep, and we took up our books and
seated ourselves in each of the parlor-windows.
Now, what do you think, papa, these books
were? Olivia's was "Sheridan's Dictionary,"
and mine was an "Essay on the Human Understanding," by Mr. Locke, gent. . . .

MISS SYDNEY OWENSON (AFTERWARDS LADY MOR-
GAN) TO HER FATHER

CASTLETOWN DELVIN, 1800.

The reason that I have not written to you
for some days is that I have so much to say
and so much that I was afraid of saying, that I
thought it better to say nothing at all ; which
" all," I think, will surprise you—and for myself *je n' en reviens pas !*

Well, last Thursday, Mr. Fontaine enclosed
me a note from a lady, Mrs. Featherstonehaugh,
of Bracklin Castle, intimating her desire to have
just such a charming young person as myself !
as governess or companion to her two daughters ; the eldest just returned from a great
finishing school, Madame Lafarrelle's, and the
younger who has never left home.

Mrs. Featherstone was for a few days at her
mother's, the Dowager Lady Steele's in Dominic Street, but anxious not to lose a moment,
and would send her carriage for the young lady
M. Lafontaine had mentioned in his letter
(Miss Owenson) if he would send her address.
And so he did, and so the carriage came—and
so I went—rather downhearted from my former
disappointments.

You know what a fine street Dominic Street is, and so close to my old school.   Well, a handsome mansion, two servants at the door, my name taken, and I was ushered at once into a large and rather gloomy parlor, in the centre of which two ladies were sitting at a table.   The one at the head of the table, a most remarkable figure both in person and costume, but who bore her ninety years with considerable confidence in her own dignity.   She sat with her head thrown back, her little sharp eyes twinkling at me as I entered, and her mouth pursed up to the dimensions of a parish poor-box. She wore a fly-cap (of which I have taken the pattern), on her silver but frizzled hair,—her very fair face was drawn into small wrinkles, as though engraved with a needle over her delicate features, and when I tell you what I have since heard, that she was the rival and friend of the beautiful Lady Palmer, the belle of Lord Chesterfield's court, and the subject of his pretty verses which you used to recite so often, you will allow that she had every right to wrinkles and the remains of beauty.*

* The occasion was this : At the court of Lord Chesterfield, when religious party spirit was symbolized in Ireland

Seated with her at the same table, and writing, was a sweet, charming, good-humored-looking lady, who got up to receive me in the most cordial manner, whilst two nice girls, the eldest already in her teens, struggled to get me a chair, and then stationed themselves one each behind their mamma and grandmamma.

Mrs. Featherstone opened the conversation by telling me that she had been a pupil of Mr. Fontaine's as her daughters were now, and that he was the best of human beings.

" That is nothing to the purpose! " said the old lady sharply. " Come to the point with this young person, as you know you have no time to lose ; " and turning to me she said : " You are very young to offer yourself for so important a situation."

The two girls looked at me as much as to say :

by the colors white or orange, as the wearer was Williamite or Jacobite, Lady Palmer, a reigning beauty and a Catholic, appeared at one of the drawing-rooms with an orange lily in her bosom. Lord Chesterfield, having kissed her fair cheek, took out his tablets and wrote the following stanza :

> " Thou little Tory ! where 's the jest,
> To wear the orange on thy breast,
> When that same lovely breast discloses
> The whiteness of the rebel roses ! "
> *Lady Morgan's Memoirs.*

Vol. III.

" Don't mind grandmamma," and Mrs. Featherstone added :

" Dear, mamma, now, you must leave Miss
Owenson to me," and then she said to me : " I
assure you, my dear, I am much prepossessed
in your favor by all that our good Fontaine has
told me of you ; and your being so merry and
musical as he tells me you are, is very much in
your favor with us, for we are rather dull and
mopy."

" But to begin," interposed Lady Steele
again. " What will this young person expect?
She cannot offer herself as a regular governess,
she is so very young."

The girls winked at me and grimaced again.

" She shall first offer herself as my visitor at
Bracklin Castle for the Christmas holidays,"
said Mrs. Featherstone, kindly, " and then we
shall see how we get on and suit each other,
which I am sure we shall very well."

The old lady said, knocking her hand on the
table, " I never heard such nonsense in all my
life ! "

At this moment the footman came in to announce that the carriage was at the door, followed by a handsome, jolly-looking woman, the

lady's maid, with Mrs. Featherstone's cloak and bonnet.

Mrs. Featherstone said: " Come, my dear, and I will set you down, and we will have a lit-tle talk by the way, for I have an appointment which hurries me away at present." The two girls ran after us and said, " Do come to us, we shall be so happy at Bracklin, and never mind grandmamma,—nobody does," and with this dutiful observation they shook hands cordially with me, and I drove off with my brand new friend. What was amusing in all this was— that I had never opened my lips till I got into the carriage, when I thanked Mrs. Feather-stone for her kind reception, and accepted cor· dially her invitation to Bracklin. In short, there was a mutual sympathy between us; the result, I believe, of mutual good-humor and good-nature. . . .

Well, it was finally arranged, I was to start for Bracklin on the following Monday (this was Friday) by the mail, which would take me as far as Kinigad, where the Featherstone carriage, horses, and servants would meet me ; but as the mail reached Kinigad at an awkward hour, I was not to leave that place till daylight. In

short, I never met any one so kind as this dear
lady.

Olivia and Molly heard all this with astonish-
ment, but agreed that it was quite right ; as did
also Dr. Pellegrini, who came with Madame
and carried us off to dinner.

The next morning I took my darling Olivia
to Madame Dacier's—

"Some natural tears we dropped, but wiped them soon,"

full of the hope of meeting next spring.

Molly came back with me to prepare all my
little arrangements, towards which we changed
our last bank note. And having next day
received all details in a letter from Mrs. Feath-
stone from Bracklin, written the night she arrived, I accepted a farewell dinner and a little
dance after, which Mr. Fontaine called a *petit bal
d'adieu* for the night of my departure; he said :
" The mail goes from the head of this street ; it
will blow its horn when it is ready for you, and
we will all conduct you to your carriage."

Well, papa, this was all very nice, for I
wanted to be cheered, so I dressed myself in my
school dancing dress, a muslin frock, and pink
silk stockings and shoes. Molly had my warm
things to change in time for the mail.

Well, dear papa, we did not exactly mind our time, and the fatal result was—that I was dancing down "Money in both Pockets" with a very nice young man, Mr. Buck, the nephew to Miss Buck, when the horn blew at the end of the street! Oh, sir! if you knew the panic! All that could be done was for Molly to throw her warm cloak over me, with my own bonnet and my little bundle of things, so that I might dress when I got to Kinigad.

One of the young gentlemen snatched up my portmanteau, and so we all flew along the flags, which were frosted over, and got to the mail just as the guard lost patience and was mounting, so I was poked in and the door banged to, and "my carriage" drove off like lightning down College Green, along the quays, and then into some gloomy street I did not remember.

As for me, I was so addled, I did not know where I was. At last we drew up before some ponderous gates and a high wall.

A sentinel was pacing up and down with a lantern flashing on his arms, which reminded me of the castle of Otranto. The guard blew his horn, and the next minute I heard an awful shout, and uproar, and singing, and laughing, and the gates opened and there appeared a crowd of officers and gentlemen, who were shaking hands with one person, with "Goodbye, old boy, and let us hear from you soon," and other phrases.

The coach door was opened, and the gentleman asked the guard, " Is there any one inside ? "

And the guard answered, " Only an old lady, sir, as far as Kinigad !"

" Oh, by Jove !" said the gentleman, retreating.   " I say, coachy, I 'll take a seat by you." So the door slapped to, up he mounted, and the horn blew, and we were off in a minute.

Oh-h, sir, it takes away my breath only to think of it now !

Well, we were soon out of Dublin ; the moon rising over the beautiful Phœnix Park, the trees of which were hanging with frost and icicles ; the Liffey glittering to the left, and lights glittering in the Viceregal Lodge as we passed it on the right.

If my heart had not been so heavy, this would have been a scene I should have delighted in.   And so we galloped on, changing horses only once, when I was much struck with the interior of the stable, which was lighted only by a lamp, but very picturesque; something one would like to paint or describe.

Our next stage was Kinigad; but it was a very long one, and we did not arrive till three in the morning.

Such a picture as the inn was! The ostler, half-dressed, coming with the horses, and roaring for a waiter, or Caty, the chambermaid, to come down; and then the officer sprang down from the coach-box and came to rummage in the coach for his hat, just as I was stepping out, assisted by the dirty ostler. I suppose the officer was struck with my pink silk shoe, for he laid hold of my foot, and, pushing back the ostler, he said:

"What! let such a foot as *that* sink in the snow—never!" and he actually carried me in his arms into the kitchen, and placed me in an old arm-chair before a roaring turf fire! and then, ordering the chambermaid and Mrs. Kearney (the landlady, I suppose) " to get up and get tea, and every thing for the young lady," to which everybody answered:

"Yes, Major; to be sure, sir; every thing

your honor orders.   Your gig has been here, sir, this hour."

In short, he seemed the commandant of the place.

He then came up to me and said :

"I had not the least idea who was in the carriage.   The guard said it was an *old lady ;* in short, you must let me make amends by offering my services in this wretched place.   I hope you will command them now.   I am quartered here, and know its few resources. You are not going further to-night, I suppose ?"

I was dreadfully frightened and confused, but I answered :

"No, sir; not at present.   I am expecting a carriage and servants to take me on to Mr. Featherstone's, of Bracklin."

He took off his hat, made me a low bow, but seemed stunned with the information.   He again called the landlady and said :

"I would prescribe some white-wine negus, for you are chilled."

The waiter now appeared, and said that Mr. Featherstone's carriage and servants had arrived an hour before ; but had put up the horses and gone to lie down, as they would not proceed till after daylight. The chambermaid now came, and said she had a room prepared and a good fire upstairs. This was a great relief to me ; but the young officer seemed to deplore it. He said he knew Mr. Featherstone, and would take the liberty of coming to inquire for me.

So I went to my smoky room; but on in-quiring for my bundle and portmanteau, I found they had gone on in the Kinigad mail.

Fancy, dear papa, my dreadful situation! My whole stock in trade consisted of a white muslin frock, pink silk stockings, and pink silk shoes, with Molly's warm cloak and an old bon-net.

Well, sir, you know I had nothing for it, so I took my glass of hot white-wine negus, threw myself on the bed, and was warmly covered up by the fat chambermaid, who had neither shoes nor stockings on, and I fell fast asleep ; " but in that sleep what dreams! " papa; from all of which I was roused by the fat chambermaid coming to tell me that Mr. Featherstone's coach-man could not wait any longer ; so I rolled Molly's cloak round me, and proceeded to Bracklin.

The dreary Irish road from Kinigad to the

pretty village of Castletown Delvin—an ap-
pendage to the domain of the Earl of Westmeath—brought me to the approach of the
pine-sheltered avenue of Bracklin, which pines,
green and formal as they were, screened out
the black bog behind them, where the wood of
ages lay buried, from among which "the mere
Irish" could never be taken by their Saxon in-
vaders "when the leaves were on the trees!"

The approach to the domain was announced
by a civilized-looking lodge; large, beautiful
iron gates, opened by a fairy child, and all that
lay within was cultivated and promising, leading to a large handsome mansion of white
stone—two carriages were rolling before the
door, at which stood two footmen, who at once
ushered me into a handsome drawing-room, to
a party of ladies, muffled in carriage dresses,
who stood in a circle round the fire. Pinched,
cold, confused, and miserable, as you may suppose, dear papa, I must have been—in my pink
silk shoes and stockings—I perceived that my
appearance excited a general titter; but dear
Mrs. Featherstone and her girls came to my
relief, and welcomed me and kissed me; but
Mr. Featherstone—a grave, stern-looking man,

who sat apart reading his newspaper—he just
raised his eyes above his glasses, and I read in
his glance condemnation of his lady's indiscre-
tion in bringing *such* a being for *such* a purpose
as I had come.

Mrs. Featherstone inquired how I had come
to travel in so light a dress ; and so, dear papa,
I thought I had better just tell the story as it
happened—and so I did—from the little *bal d'
adieu*, at dear old Fontaine's, till I reached
Bracklin gates, not forgetting the portmanteau
and little bundle left behind. Well, you have
no idea how it took ! they screamed at the fun
of my details, and I heard them mutter : " Dear
little thing—poor little thing ! " The two girls
carried me off from them all, to my own rooms,
the prettiest suite you *ever* saw—a study, a
bedroom, and a bathroom—a roaring turf fire in
the rooms, and an open piano and lots of books
scattered about !

Betty Kenny, the old nurse—the " Molly "
of the establishment—brought me in a bowl of
laughing potatoes, and *such* fresh butter, and
gave a hearty " much good may it do you,
miss "; and did n't I tip her a word of Irish
which delighted her. Pen, ink, and paper were

brought me, and I was left to myself to rest and write to dear Olivia a line just to announce my arrival here, which was sent to the post for me.

The girls brought me, I believe, half their mamma's and all their own wardrobe, to dress me out; and as they are all little, it answered very well. Well, sir, when I went down, the carriages and party had drawn off to spend two days at Sir Thomas Featherstone's.

Our dinner party were mamma and the two young ladies, two itinerant preceptors—Mr. O'Hanlon, a writing and elocution master, and a dancing-master, and Father Murphy, the P.P. —such fun! and the Rev. Mr. Beaufort, the curate of Castletown Delvin.

Now I must just give you a picture of the room. A beautiful dining-room—spacious and lofty; a grand buffet and sideboard; before it stood Mr. James Moran, the butler—the drollest fellow I ever met, as I will tell you, by-and-by—and two footmen.

The dinner, perfectly delicious!

Well, I was in great spirits; and Mrs. Featherstone drew out the two tutors, I think, on purpose. She made Mr. O'Hanlon—a most

coxcombical writing-master—tell me his story ;
how he was the prince of nearly all he surveyed
—if he had his rights, being descended from the
Princes O'Hanlon. Now, papa, *you* know if
there is any thing I am strong on it is Irish
song—thanks to you—especially " Emunch ach
Nuic " (Ned o' the Hills), which song I sang
for them afterwards, by-the-by, and did I not
take his pride down a peg, and get him into
such a passion ! The servants laughed and
stuffed their napkins down their throats till
they were almost suffocated. James Moran,
the butler, winking at the priest all the time,
who enjoyed the joke more than any one, except the dancing-master, his rival, who is a very
clever man, I am told, and teaches mathematics
besides, and put me very much in mind of
Marcus Tully. Well, sir, we got so merry, that
at last Father Murphy proposed my health in
this fashion—which will make you smile. He
stood up with his glass of port wine in his hand,
and first bowing to Mrs. Featherstone, said :
" With your lave, madam " ; and then turning
to me, he said : " This is a hearty welcome to
ye, to Westmeath, Miss Owenson ; and this is
to your health, mind and body," which made

them all laugh till they were ready to fall under the table.

Well, after dinner I sang them " Emunch ach Nuic," and " Cruel Barbara Allen," which had an immense effect.

After tea, James Moran announced that the piper had come from Castletown " to play in Miss Owenson," upon which the girls immediately proposed a dance in the back hall; and when I told them I was a famous jig dancer, they were perfectly enraptured. So we set to; all the servants crowding round two open doors in the hall.

I, of course, danced with the " Professor," and Prince O'Hanlon with Miss Featherstone, and Miss Margaret with the Rev. Mr. Beaufort. It is a pity we had no spectators beyond the domestics, for we all really danced beautifully; and, considering this was my first jig in company, I came off with flying colors, and so ends my first day in Bracklin. And I think, dear papa, you have no longer any reason to be uneasy at my position or angry with my determination, and so God bless you. I shall write to you once a-week, loving you better and better every day.

MISS MARIA EDGEWORTH TO ——

LEICESTER, 1802.

Handsome town, good shops. Walked, whilst dinner was getting ready, to a circulating library. My father asked for "Belinda," "Bulls," etc.: found they were in good repute; "Castle Rackrent," in better—the others often borrowed, but "Castle Rackrent" often bought. The bookseller, an open-hearted man, begged us to look at a book of poems just published by a Leicester lady, a Miss Watts. I recollected to have seen some years ago a specimen of this lady's proposed translation of Tasso, which my father had highly admired. He told the bookseller that we would pay our respects to Miss Watts, if it would be agreeable to her. When we had dined we set out with our enthusiastic bookseller. We were shown by the light of a lantern along a very narrow passage between high walls, to the door of a decent-looking house; a maid-servant, candle in hand, received us. "Be pleased, ladies, to walk up-stairs." A neatish room, nothing extraordinary in it except the inhabitants: Mrs. Watts, a tall, black-eyed, prim, dragon-looking woman, in the background; Miss Watts, a tall young lady in white, fresh color, fair, thin, oval face, rather pretty. The moment Mrs. Edgeworth entered, Miss Watts, taking her for the authoress, darted forward with arms, long thin arms, outstretched to their utmost swing. "Oh, what an honor this is!" each word and syllable rising in tone till the last reached a scream. Instead of embracing my mother, as her first action threatened, she started back to the farthest end of the room, which was not light enough to show her attitude distinctly, but it seemed to be intended to express the receding of awestruck admiration—stopped by the wall. Charlotte and I passed by unnoticed, and seated ourselves, by the old lady's desire; she, after many twistings of her wrists, elbows, and neck, all of which appeared to be dislocated, fixed herself in her armchair, resting her hands on the black mahogany splayed elbows. Her person was no sooner at rest than her eyes and all her features began to move in all directions. She looked like a nervous and suspicious person electrified. She seemed to be the acting partner of this house, to watch over her treasure of a daughter, to supply her with worldly wisdom, to look upon her as a phœnix, and—scold her.

Miss Watts was all ecstacy and lifting up of hands and eyes, speaking always in that loud, shrill, theatrical tone with which a puppet-master supplies his puppets. I all the time sat like a mouse. My father asked : " Which of those ladies, madam, do you think is your sister-authoress ? " " I am no physiognomist "—in a screech—" but I do imagine that to be the lady," bowing, as she sat, almost to the ground, and pointing to Mrs. Edgeworth. " No ; guess again." "Then that must be she " bowing, to Charlotte. " No." " Then this lady," looking forward to see what sort of an animal I was, for she had never seen me until this instant. To make me some amends, she now drew her chair close to me and began to pour forth praises : " ' Lady Delacour,' oh! ' Letters for Literary Ladies,' oh!" . . .

MISS FRANCES BURNEY TO HER SISTER, MRS. PHILLIPS.

February, 1782.

I thank you most heartily for your two sweet letters, my ever dearest Susy, and equally for the kindness they contain and the kindness they accept. And, as I have a frank and a subject, I will leave my *bothers*, and write you

and my dear brother Molesworth a little account of a *rout* I have just been at, at the house
of Mr. Paradise. . . .

Mrs. Paradise, leaning over the Kirwans and
Charlotte, who hardly got a seat all night for
the crowd, said she begged to speak to me. I
squeezed my great person out, and she then
said,—

" Miss Burney, Lady Say and Sele desires the
honor of being introduced to you."

Her ladyship stood by her side. She seems
pretty near fifty—at least turned forty; her
head was full of feathers, flowers, jewels, and
gewgaws, and as high as Lady Archer's; her
dress was trimmed with beads, silver, Persian
sashes, and all sorts of fine fancies; her face is
thin and fiery, and her whole manner spoke a
lady all alive.

" Miss Burney," cried she, with great quick-
ness, and a look all curiosity, " I am very happy
to see you ; I have longed to see you a great
while ; I have read your performance, and I am
quite delighted with it. I think it's the most
elegant novel I ever read in my life. Such a
style ! I am quite surprised at it. I can't think
where you got so much invention ! "

You may believe this was not a reception to make me very loquacious. I did not know which way to turn my head.

" I must introduce you," continued her ladyship, " to my sister; she 'll be quite delighted to see you. She has written a novel herself; so you are sister authoresses. A most elegant thing it is, I assure you ; almost as pretty as yours, only not quite so elegant. She has written two novels, only one is not so pretty as the other. But I shall insist upon your seeing them. One is in letters, like yours, only yours is prettiest ; it 's called the ' Mausoleum of Julia.' "

What unfeeling things, thought I, are *my* sisters ! I 'm sure I never heard them go about thus praising *me* !

Mrs. Paradise then again came forward, and taking my hand, led me up to her ladyship's sister, Lady Hawke, saying aloud, and with a courteous smirk : " Miss Burney, ma'am, authoress of ' Evelina.' "

" Yes," cried my friend, Lady Say and Sele, who followed me close, " it 's the authoress of ' Evelina ' ; so you are sister authoresses ! "

Lady Hawke arose and courtesied. She is

much younger than her sister, and rather pretty; extremely languishing, delicate, and pathetic; apparently accustomed to be reckoned the genius of her family, and well contented to be looked upon as a creature dropped from the clouds.

I was then seated between their ladyships, and Lady S. and S., drawing as near to me as possible, said :

" Well, and so you wrote this pretty book !—and pray, did your papa know of it ? "

" No, ma'am ; not till some months after the publication."

" So I 've heard ; it 's surprising ! I can't think how you invented it !—there 's a vast deal of invention in it ! And you 've got so much humor too ! Now, my sister has no humor—hers is all sentiment. You can't think how I was entertained with that old grandmother and her son ! "

I suppose she meant Tom Brangton for the son.

" How much pleasure you must have had in writing it ; had not you ? "

" Y–e–s, ma'am."

" So has my sister ; she 's never without a pen in her hand ; she can't help writing for her

life. When Lord Hawke is travelling about
with her, she keeps writing all the way."

" Yes," said Lady Hawke ; " I really can 't
help writing. One has great pleasure in writing
the things ; has not one, Miss Burney?"

" Y–e–s, ma'am."

" But your novel," cried Lady Say and Sele,
" is in such a style !—so elegant ! I am vastly
glad you made it end happily. I hate a novel
that don't end happy."

" Yes," said Lady Hawke, with a languid
smile, " I was vastly glad when she married
Lord Orville. I was sadly afraid it would not
have been."

" My sister intends," said Lady Say and Sele,
'to print her ' Mausoleum,' just for her own
friends and acquaintances."

" Yes," said Lady Hawke, " I have never
printed yet."

" I saw Lady Hawke's name," quoth I to my
first friend, " ascribed to the play of ' Variety.' "

" Did you indeed?" cried Lady Say, in an
ecstasy. " Sister ! do you know Miss Burney
saw your name in the newspapers, about the
play ! "

" Did she ? " said Lady Hawke, smiling complacently. "But I really did not write it; I never wrote a play in my life."

"Well," cried Lady Say, "but do repeat that sweet part that I am so fond of—you know what I mean; Miss Burney *must* hear it,—out of your novel, you know!"

Lady H.—No, I can't; I have forgot it.

Lady S.—Oh, no! I am sure you have not; I insist upon it.

Lady H.—But I know you can repeat it yourself; you have so fine a memory; I am sure you can repeat it.

Lady S.—Oh, but I should not do it justice! that 's all.—I should not do it justice!"

Lady Hawke then bent forward, and repeated: "'If, when he made the declaration of his love, the sensibility that beamed in his eyes was felt in his heart, what pleasing sensations and soft alarms might not that tender avowal awaken!'"

"And from what, ma'am," cried I, astonished, and imagining I had mistaken them, "is this taken?"

"From my sister's novel!" answered the delighted Lady Say and Sele, expecting my raptures to be equal to her own; "it 's in the

' Mausoleum,' ; did not you know that ? Well,
I can't think how you can write these sweet
novels ! And it 's all just like that part. Lord
Hawke himself says it 's all poetry. For my
part, I 'm sure I never could write so. I suppose, Miss Burney, you are producing another?
—aint you ? "

" No, ma'am."

" Oh, I dare say you are. I dare say you are
writing one at this very minute ! "

Mrs. Paradise now came up to me again, followed by a square man, middle-aged and hum-
drum, who I found was Lord Say and Sele,
afterwards from the Kirwans ; for though they
introduced him to me, I was so confounded by
their vehemence and their manners that I did
not hear his name.

" Miss Burney," said Mrs. P., presenting me
to him, " authoress of ' Evelina.' "

" Yes," cried Lady Say and Sele, starting up,
" 't is the authoress of ' Evelina.' "

" Of what ? " cried he.

" Of ' Evelina.' You 'd never think it, she
looks so young, to have so much invention,
and such an elegant style ! Well, I could write
a play, I think, but I 'm sure I could never
write a novel."

"Oh, yes, you could, if you would try," said Lady Hawke.

"Oh, no, I could not," answered she; "I could not get a style; that 's the thing. I could not tell how to get a style! and a novel 's nothing without a style, you know!"

"Why, no," said Lady Hawke; "that 's true. But then you write such charming letters, you know!"

"Letters," repeated Lady S. and S., simpering; "do you think so? Do you know I wrote a long letter to Mrs. Ray just before I came here, this very afternoon—quite a long letter! I did, I assure you!"

Here Mrs. Paradise came forward with another gentleman, younger, slimmer, and smarter, and saying to me: "Sir Gregory Page Turner," said to him: "Miss Burney, authoress of 'Evelina.'"

At which Lady Say and Sele, in fresh transport, again arose and rapturously again repeated: "Yes, she 's authoress of 'Evelina!' Have you read it?"

"No; is it to be had?"

"Oh, dear, yes. It 's been printed these two years! You 'd never think it! But it 's the most elegant novel I ever read in my life. Writ in such a style!"

"Certainly," said he, very civilly; "I have every inducement to get it. Pray, where is it to be had?—everywhere, I suppose?"

"Oh, nowhere, I hope!" cried I, wishing at that moment it had been never in human ken.

My *square* friend, Lord Say and Sele, then putting his head forward, said, very solemnly: "I'll purchase it!"

His lady then mentioned to me a hundred novels that I had never heard of, asking my opinion of them, and whether I knew the authors, Lady Hawke only occasionally and languidly joining in the discourse, and then Lady S. and S., suddenly arising, begged me not to move, for she should be back again in a minute, and flew to the next room.

I took, however, the first opportunity of Lady Hawke casting down her eyes, and re-clining her delicate head, to make away from this terrible set, and just as I was got up by the piano-forte, where I hoped Pacchierotti would soon present himself, Mrs. Paradise again came to me and said:

"Miss Burney, Lady Say and Sele wishes

vastly to cultivate your acquaintance, and begs
to know if she may have the honor of your
company to an assembly at her house next
Friday, and I will do myself the pleasure to call
for you, if you will give me leave."

"Her ladyship does me much honor, but I
am unfortunately engaged," was my answer,
with as much promptness as I could command.

WHIM AND FANCY.

LADY DUFFERIN TO MISS BERRY.

HAMPTON HALL, DORCHESTER, 1846.

Your kind little note followed me here, dear
Miss Berry, which must account for my not
having answered it sooner. As you guessed, I
was obliged to follow my "*things*" (as the
maids always call their raiment) into the jaws
of the law. I think the Old Bailey is a charming place. We were introduced to a live Lord
Mayor, and I sat between two Sheriffs. The
Common Serjeant talked to me familiarly, and
I am not sure that the Governor of Newgate
did not call me " Nelly." As for the Rev. Mr.
Carver (the ordinary), if the inherent vanity of
my sex does not mislead me, I *think* I have
made a deep impression there. Altogether, my
Old Bailey recollections are of the most pleasing and gratifying nature. It is true that I
have only got back three pairs and a half of
stockings, one gown, and two shawls ; but that
is but a trifling consideration in studying the
glorious institutions of our country. We were

treated with the greatest respect, and ham sandwiches; and two magistrates handed us down to the carriage. For my part, I could not think we were in the *criminal* court, as the law was so uncommonly *civil.* . . . . My mother and I have returned to this place for a few days, in order to make an ineffectual grasp upon any *remaining* property that we may have in the world. Of course, you have heard that we were robbed and murdered the other night by a certain soft-spoken cook, who headed a storming party of banditti through my mother's kitchen window; if not, you will see the full, true, and dreadful particulars in the papers, as we are to be "had up" at the Old Bailey on Monday next for the trial. We have seen a great deal of life, and learned a great deal of the criminal law of England this week—knowledge cheaply purchased at the cost of all my wardrobe and all my mother's plate. We have gone through two examinations in court; they were very hurrying and agitating affairs, and I had to kiss either the Bible or the magistrate, I don't recollect which, but *it* smelt of thumbs. The magistrates seemed to take less interest in my clothes than in my mother's spoons—I suppose from secret *affinity* or *congeniality,* which

they were conscious of, *similis gaudet*, something (I have lost my Latin with the rest of my
property). When I say "similis," I don't so
much allude to the purity of the metal, as to
its particular form.

I find that the idea of *personal property* is a
fascinating illusion, for our goods belong in fact
to our country and not to us; and that the
petticoats and stockings I have fondly imagined
mine, are really the petticoats of Great Britain
and Ireland. I am now and then indulged with
a distant glimpse of my most necessary gar-
ments in the hands of different policemen; but
" in this stage of the proceedings" may do no
more than wistfully recognize them. Even on
such occasions, the words of Justice are:
" Policeman B. 25, produce *your* gowns." " Letter A. 36, identify *your* lace." " Letter C, tie
up *your* stockings." All this is harrowing to
the feelings, but one cannot have every thing
in this life. We have obtained *justice*, and can
easily wait for a change of linen. Hopes are
held out to us, that at some vague period in
the lapse of time we may be allowed a *wear*
out of our raiment—at least so much of it as
may have resisted the wear and tear of justice;
and my poor mother looks confidently forward

to being restored to the bosom of her silver
teapot. But I don't know! I begin to look
upon all property with a philosophic eye, as un-
stable in its nature, and liable to all sorts of
pawnbrokers ; moreover, the police and I have
so long had my clothes in common, that I shall
never feel at home in them again. To a virtuous mind the idea that " Inspector Dousett "
examined into all one's hooks and eyes, tapes
and buttons, etc., is inexpressibly painful. But
I cannot pursue that view of the subject. Let
me hope, dear Miss Berry, that you feel for us
as we really deserve, and that you wish me well
"thro' my clothes" on Monday next! If I
were sure you are at Richmond still, I might
endeavor to return your kind visit; but at
present our costumes are too *light* and our
hearts too heavy for the empty forms and cere-
monies of social intercourse. I hope, however,
to see you ere long; and with very kind re-
membrances to your sister, believe me, yours
very truly.

_____

CHARLES DICKENS TO MRS. WATSON.

BROADSTAIRS, KENT, July 11, 1851.

. . . I find I am " used up " by the exhibition.* I don't say " there is nothing in it "—

* The Crystal Palace.

there 's too much.   I have only been twice : so
many things bewilder me.   I have a natural
horror of sights, and the fusion of so many
sights in one has not decreased it.   I am not
sure that I have seen any thing but the fountain, and perhaps the Amazon.   It is a dreadful thing to be obliged to be false, but when
any one says: " Have you seen —— ? " I say :
" Yes," because if I don't I know he 'll explain
it, and I can't bear that.   —— took all the
school one day.   The school was composed of
a hundred "infants," who got among the
horses' legs in coming to the main entrance from the Kensington Gate, and came
walking from between the wheels of coaches undisturbed in mind.   They were clinging to
horses, I am told, all over the park.

When they were collected and added up by
the frantic monitors, they were all right.   They
were then regaled with cake, etc., and went
tottering and staring all over the place ; the
greater part wetting their forefingers and drawing a wavy pattern on every accessible object.
One infant strayed.   He was not missed.
Ninety and nine were taken home, supposed to
be the whole collection, but this particular in-

fant went to Hammersmith. He was found by
the police at night, going round and round the
turnpike, which he still supposed to be a part
of the Exhibition.   He had the same opinion
of the police, also of Hammersmith workhouse,
where he passed the night.   When his mother
came for him in the morning, he asked when it
would be over.   It was a great exhibition, he
said, but he thought it long. . . .

———

WILLIAM COWPER TO JOHN NEWTON.

OLNEY, November 30, 1783.

. . . I have wondered in former days at the
patience of the antediluvian world ; that they
could endure a life almost millenary, with so
little variety as seems to have fallen to their
share. It is probable that they had much
fewer employments than we.   Their affairs
lay in a narrower compass ; their libraries were
indifferently furnished ; philosophical researches
were carried on with much less industry and
acuteness of penetration, and fiddles, perhaps,
were not even invented.   How then could
seven or eight hundred years of life be support-
able ? I have asked this question formerly,

and been at a loss to resolve it ; but I think I can answer it now. I will suppose myself born a thousand years before Noah was born or thought of. I rise with the sun ; I worship ; I prepare my breakfast ; I swallow a bucket of goat's milk, and a dozen good sizeable cakes. I fasten a new string to my bow, and my youngest boy, a lad of about thirty years of age, having played with my arrows till he has stript off all the feathers, I find myself obliged to repair them. The morning is thus spent in pre-paring for the chase, and it is become necessary that I should dine. I dig up my roots ; I wash them ; I boil them ; I find them not done enough ; I boil them again ; my wife is angry ; we dispute ; we settle the point ; but in the meantime the fire goes out, and must be kindled again. All this is very amusing. I hunt ; I bring home the prey ; with the skin of it I mend an old coat, or I make a new one. By this time the day is far spent ; I feel myself fatigued, and retire to rest. Thus what with tilling the ground and eating the fruit of it, hunting and walking, and running, and mending old clothes, and sleeping, and rising again, I can suppose an inhabitant of the primeval world so much occupied as to sigh over the shortness of life, and to find at the end of many centuries that they had all slipt though his fingers, and were passed away like a shadow. What wonder, then, that I, who live in a day of so much greater refinement, when there is so much more to be wanted, and wished, and to be enjoyed, should feel myself now and then pinched in point of opportunity, and at some loss for leisure to fill four sides of a sheet like this ? . . .

NORMAN MACLEOD TO HIS MOTHER.

JUNE 3, 1868.

I am quite safe in saying that I have written to you, say forty letters, on my birthday; and whatever was defective as to number in my letters was made up by your love. Now I begin to think the whole affair is getting stale to you. In short you anticipate all I can say, am likely to say, or ought to say; and having done so, you begin to read and to laugh and cry time about, and to praise me to all my unfortunate brothers and sisters, until they detest me till June 4th. Don't you feel grateful I was

born? Are you not thankful? I know you are,
and no wonder. I need not enumerate all those
well-known personal and domestic virtues which
have often called forth your praises, except
when you are beaten at backgammon. But
there is another side of the question with which
I have to do, and that is, whether I ought to be
so very grateful to you for the event with
which June 3, 1812, is associated. As I ad-
vance in life, this question becomes more interesting to me; and it seems due to the interests
of truth and justice to state on this day, when
I have had fifty-six years' experience of life in
its most varied forms, that I am by no means
satisfied with your conduct on that occasion,
and that if you fairly consider it, I feel assured
you will justify me in demanding from you the
only reparation possible—an ample apology,
and a solemn promise never to do the like again!
You must acknowledge that you took a very
great liberty with a man of my character and
position, not to ask me whether I was disposed
to enter upon a new and important state of existence; whether I should prefer winter or
summer to begin the trial; or whether I should
be a Scotchman, Irishman or Englishman; or

even whether I should be "man or woman born"; each of these alternatives involving to me most important consequences. What a good John Bull I would have made! what a rattling, roaring Irishman! what a capital mother or wife! what a jolly abbess! But you doomed me to be born in a tenth-rate provincial town, half Scotch, half Highland, and sealed my doom as to sex and country. Was that fair? Would you like me to have done that to you? Suppose through my fault you had been born a wild Spanish papist, what would you have said on your fifty-seventh birthday, with all your Protestant convictions? Not one Maxwell or Buntroon related to you! you yourself a nun called St. Agnese!—and all, forsooth, because I had willed that you should be born at Toledo on June 3, 1812! Think of it, mother, seriously, and say, have you done to me as you would have had me do to you?

Then, again, pray who is to blame for all I have suffered for fifty-six years? Who but you? This reply alone can be made to a thousand questions which press themselves on my memory, until the past seems a history of misery endured with angelic patience. Why, I might

ask, for example, did I live for weeks on insipid
"lythings," spending days and nights screaming, weeping, hiccoughing, with an old woman
swathing and unswathing me, whose nature re-
tires from such attentions? Why had I for
years to learn to walk and speak, and amuse
aunts and friends like a young parish fool, and
wear frocks—fancy me in a frock now, address-
ing the Assembly! and yet I had to wear them
for years! Why have I suffered from mumps,
hooping-cough, measles, scarlet-fever, toothache, headache, lumbago, gout, sciatica, sore
back, sore legs, sore sides, and other ailments;
having probably sneezed several thousand
times, and coughed as often since christened?
Why? Because I was born! because you, and
none but you, insisted I should be born! Why
have I had to be tossed about on every sea and
ocean, and kept in perpetual danger from ice-
bergs, fogs, storms, shipwrecks? You did it!
Why have I had my mind distracted, my brain
worn, my heart broken, my nerves torn, my
frame exhausted, my life tortured with preach-
ings and preparations, speeches, lectures, mo-
tions, resolutions, programmes; with sessions,
presbyteries, and assemblies; with all churches,

bond and free; with all countries from west to east, with good words and bad words; with Sunday questions and week-day questions; with all sorts of people, from Trembling Jock to the Queen; with friends and relations, Jews and Greeks, bond and free? Why all this, and a thousand times more, if not simply and solely because, forsooth, of your conduct on June 3, 1812? No wonder it is a solemn and sad day to you! No wonder you sigh, and—unless all good is out of you—weep too. I was told my poor father, on the day I was born, hid himself in a hayrick from sheer anxiety. He had some idea of what was doing. But, dear soul! he always gave in to you, and it was in vain for either of us to speak. I am told I yelled very loud—I hope I did—I could do no more then; and I can do little more now than protest, as I do, against the whole arrangement.

An American expressed to a friend of mine a great desire to visit Siam, as he understood its people were all twins! The thought makes me tremble. What if I had been born like the Siamese twins! Think of my twin brother and myself going as a deputy to India; in the same berth, speaking together at the same meeting,

sick together at sea, or both suffering from
gout, and you concerned and anxious about
your poor, dear boys! What, supposing my
twin had married Mrs. ——?

Mother, dear, repent!

One good quality remains: I can forgive,
and I do forgive you this day, in pledge of
which I send you my love, big as my body, yea
without limit, as large a kiss as my beard and
moustache will permit. . . .

LORD EDWARD FITZGERALD TO HIS MOTHER.

FREDERICK'S TOWN, NEW BRUNSWICK,
September 2, 1788.

. . . I know Ogilvie says I ought to have
been a savage; and if it were not that the
people I love and wish to live with are civilized people, and like houses, etc., etc., I really
would join the savages; and, leaving all our
fictitious, ridiculous wants, be what nature intended we should be. Savages have all the
real happiness of life, without any of those in-
conveniences, or ridiculous obstacles to it, which
custom has introduced among us. They enjoy
the love and company of their wives, relations,
and friends, without any interference of interests or ambition to separate them. To bring

things home to one's self, if *we* had been Indians, instead of its being my duty to be separated from all of you, it would, on the contrary, be my duty to be with you, to make you
comfortable, and to hunt and fish for you: instead of Lord ——'s being violent against letting me marry G——, he would be glad to give
her to me, that I might maintain and feed her.
There would be then no cases of looking forward to the fortune for children,—of thinking
how you are to live: no separations in families, one in Ireland, one in England: no devil-
ish politics, no fashions, customs, duties, or
appearances to the world, to interfere with
one's happiness. Instead of being served and
supported by servants, every thing here is done
by one's relations—by the people one loves;
and the mutual obligations you must be under
increase your love for each other. To be sure,
the poor ladies are obliged to cut a little wood
and bring a little water. Now the dear Ciss
and Mimi, instead of being with Mrs. Lynch,
would be carrying wood and fetching water,
while ladies Lucy and Sophia were cooking or
drying fish. As for you, dear mother, you
would be smoking your pipe. Ogilvie and us

boys, after having brought in our game, would be lying about the fire, while our squaws were helping the ladies to cook, or taking care of our papooses : all this in a fine wood, beside some beautiful lake, which when you were tired of, you would in ten minutes, without any baggage, get into your canoes, and off with you elsewhere. . . .

BISHOP CONNOP THIRLWALL TO ——

ABERGWILI PALACE, November 19, 1867.

. . . " Oh, but it is a blessed doctrine," said a pious Scotch lady, speaking of the dogma of the total depravity of mankind, " if folk wad only live up til it ! " What, you will ask, could put that anecdote into your head ? and to what is it *à-propos* ? Well, it is *à-propos* to your vexation at having your rest broken, and missing the sight of the fiery shower which may have been so glorious to behold, after all. But what has the meteoric shower to do with human depravity? and how did it put the Scotchwoman's remark into your head? Alas! it was my own evil conscience that formed the associating link. You who would make me believe that I am very nearly perfect will be astonished to hear how I have been illustrating

the " blessed doctrine." I ought, of course, to
have felt nothing but concern for your disappointment.   Instead of this it occurred to me
that I had also wished very much to see the
meteors, and had intended to watch for them,
but entirely forgot them until I received your
letter, and then, instead of sympathizing with
your annoyance—will you believe it possible?
—I actually caught myself pleased with the
thought that if I had watched it would have
been to no purpose, and that I lost no spectacle which in these parts was visible to anybody. Is it easily possible for human depravity
to go beyond that?   On the other hand, I remember that I was very much amazed by the
descriptions I heard of the magnificent spectacle which I missed through my. stupid
thoughtlessness last August.   You may pass
these things over lightly, but I am sure that
the Scotchwoman would have considered them
as striking examples of her doctrine. . . .

RICHARD HARRIS BARHAM TO HIS DAUGHTER.

WANDSWORTH, August, 1839.

Your brother has got a black coat, and your
cat a black kitten, and it 's dead—not the coat,

nor the cat, but the kitten; there were seven, and one was preserved, and so were seven pots of raspberry jam; and Ned has got a donkey, and he is quite plump and fat—not the donkey, but Ned; and I am going a-fishing, and they are fiddling outside the window, and we caught eight dozen and a half of gudgeons last Wednesday, and the Chartists have been to St. Paul's, and Dick preached yesterday at St. Gregory's, and Mary Anne has got the oil cruet to dress her doll's wig with; and they are making such a noise that I can't hear myself write, so your mamma must tell you the rest of the news, and God bless you, and Mr. Mole, that is, the coachman, and bid him take care of you, and believe me your most affectionate Father.

THOMAS HOOD TO A CHILD.

DEVONSHIRE LODGE, NEW FINCHLEY ROAD,
July 1, 1844.

So you are at Sandgate! Of course, wishing for your old play-fellow, M—— H—— (he *can* play,—it 's work to me), to help you to make little puddles in the Sand, and swing on the Gate. But perhaps there are no sand and gate at Sandgate, which, in that case, nominally tells us a fib. But there must be little crabs somewhere, which you can catch, if you are nimble enough, so like spiders, I wonder they do not make webs. The large crabs are scarcer.

If you do catch a big one with strong claws —and like experiments,—you can shut him up in a cupboard with a loaf of sugar, and you can see whether he will break it up with his nippers. Besides crabs, I used to find jelly-fish on the beach, made, it seemed to me, of sea-calves' feet, and no sherry.

The mermaids eat them, I suppose, at their wet water-parties, or salt *soirées.*

I suppose you never gather any sea-flowers, but only sea-weeds. The truth is, Mr. David Jones never rises from his bed, and so has a garden full of weeds, like Dr. Watts' Sluggard. . . .

I have heard that you bathe in the sea, which is very refreshing, but it requires care; for if you stay under water too long you may come up a mermaid, who is only half a lady, with a fish's tail,—which she can boil if she likes. You had better try this with your doll, whether it turns her into half a "dollfin."

I hope you like the sea. I always did

when I was a child, which was about two years ago. Sometimes it makes such a fizzing and foaming, I wonder some of our London cheats do not bottle it up, and sell it for ginger-pop. . . .

Some time ago exactly, there used to be, about the part of the coast where you are, large white birds with black-tipped wings, that went flying and screaming over the sea, and now and then plunged down into the water after a fish. Perhaps they catch their sprats now with nets or hooks and lines. Do you ever see such birds? We used to call thom "gulls,"—but they did n't mind it! Do you ever see any boats or vessels? And don't you wish, when you see a ship, that somebody was a sea-captain instead of a doctor, that he might bring you home a pet lion, or calf elephant, ever so many parrots, or a monkey, from foreign parts? I knew a little girl who was promised a baby whale by her sailor brother, and who *blubbered* because he did not bring it. I suppose there are no whales at Sandgate, but you might find a seal about the beach ; or, at least, a stone for one. The sea stones are not pretty when they are dry, but look beautiful when they are wet, and we can *always* keep sucking them!

If you can find one, pray pick me up a pebble for a seal. I prefer the red sort, like Mrs. Jenkins' brooch and ear-rings, which she calls "red chamelion." Well, how happy you must be! Childhood is such a joyous, merry time; and I often wish I was two or three children! But I suppose I can't be; or else I would be Jeanie, and May, and Dunnie Elliot. And would n't I pull off my three pairs of shoes and socks, and go paddling in the sea up to my six knees! And oh! how I could climb up the downs, and roll down the ups on my three backs and stomachs! . . .

THOMAS HOOD TO A CHILD.

DEVONSHIRE LODGE, NEW FINCHLEY ROAD,
July 1, 1844.

How do you do? and how do you like the sea? Not much, perhaps; it 's "so big." But should n't you like a nice little ocean that you could put in a pan? . . .

I remember that, when I saw the sea, it used sometimes to be very fussy, and fidgetty, and did not always wash itself quite clean; but it was very fond of fun. Have the waves ever run after you yet, and turned your little two shoes into pumps, full of water? . . .

Did you ever taste the sea-water? The fishes are so fond of it they keep drinking it all the day long. Dip your little finger in, and then suck it to see how it tastes. A glass of it warm, with sugar, and a grate of nutmeg, would quite astonish you! The water of the sea is so saline I wonder nobody catches salt fish in it. I should think a good way would be to go out in a butter-boat, with a little melted for sauce. Have you been bathed yet in the sea, and were you afraid? I was, the first time, and the time before that; and, dear me, how I kicked and screamed—or, at least, meant to scream, but the sea, ships and all, began to run into my mouth, and so I shut it up. I think I see *you* being dipped in the sea, screwing your eyes up, and putting your nose, like a button, into your mouth, like a button-hole, for fear of getting another smell and taste! By the bye, did you ever dive your head under water with your legs up in the air like a duck, and try whether you could cry "Quack"? Some animals can! I would try, but there is no sea here, and so I am forced to dip into books. I wish there were

such nice green hills here as there are at Sandgate. They must be very nice to roll down,
especially if there are no furze bushes to prickle
one at the bottom !   Do you remember how
the thorns stuck in us like a penn'orth of
mixed pins at Wanstead ?   I have been very
ill, and am so thin now I could stick myself
into a prickle.   My legs, in particular, are so
wasted away that somebody says my pins are
only needles; and I am so weak, I dare say you
could push me down on the floor, and right
through the carpet, unless it was a strong pattern.
I am sure if I were at Sandgate you could
carry me to the post-office, and fetch my letters.   Talking of carrying, I suppose you have
donkeys at Sandgate, and ride about on them.
Mind and always call them " donkeys," for if
you call them asses, it might reach such long
ears ! I knew a donkey once that kicked a man
for calling him Jack instead of John.

   There are no flowers, I suppose, on the
beach, or I would ask you to bring me a bou-
quet, as you used at Stratford.   But there
are little crabs !   If you would catch one for
me and teach it to dance the polka, it would
make me quite happy ; for I have not had any

toys or playthings for a long time. Did you ever try, like a little crab, to run two ways at once? See if you can do it, for it is good fun; never mind tumbling over yourself a little at first. It would be a good plan to hire a little crab, for an hour a day, to teach baby to crawl, if he can't walk, and, if I was his mamma, I *would* too! Bless him! But I must not write on him any more—he is so soft, and I have nothing but steel pens.

And now good-bye; Fanny has made my tea, and I must drink it before it gets too hot, as we *all* were last Sunday week. They say the glass was 88 in the shade, which is a great age! The last fair breeze I blew dozens of kisses for you, but the wind changed, and, I am afraid, took them all to Miss H——, or somebody that it should n't. Give my love to everybody, and my compliments to all the rest. . . .

SYDNEY SMITH TO LADY DUFFERIN.

COMBE FLOREY (no date).

I am just beginning to get well from that fit of gout, at the beginning of which you were charitable enough to pay me a visit—and I said the same Providence which inflicts gout creates

Dufferins! We must take the good and the
evils of life.

I am charmed, I confess, with the beauty of
this country. I hope some day you will be
charmed with it too. It banished, however,
every Arcadian notion to see —— walk in at
the gate to-day. I seemed to be transported
instantly to Piccadilly, and the innocence went
out of me.

I hope the process of furnishing goes on well.
Attend, I pray you, to the proper selection of
an easy-chair, where you may cast yourself
down, in the weariness and distresses of life,
with the absolute certainty that every joint of
the human frame will receive all the comfort which can be derived from an easy
position and soft materials; then the glass on
which your eyes are so often fixed, knowing
that you have the great duty imposed on the
Sheridans of looking well. You may depend
upon it, happiness depends mainly on these
little things.

I hope you remain in perfect favor with
Rogers, and that you are not omitted in any of
the dress breakfast parties. Remember me to
the Norton: tell her I am glad to be sheltered
from her beauty by the insensibility of age;

that I shall not live to see its decay, but die
with that unfaded image before my eyes. . . .

SYDNEY SMITH TO MISS MARY BERRY.

COMBE FLOREY, August 28, 1844.

The general notion here is that the two Miss
Berrys, in conjunction with Lady Charlotte,
have been destroyed by fire at Richmond. I
am told that the Hand-in-Hand and the
Phœnix fire-engines played upon them for a
considerable time without the smallest effect ;
that they were so brilliant, and emitted so
many sparks, and showed themselves to be
composed of materials so combustible, that it
was impossible to save them ; that the elder
Miss Berry (Elder Berry) was heard, in her last
sufferings, inviting a party to dinner after the
fire. Lady Charlotte, with her glass, eyed to
the last moment the fire people who were playing upon her ; and Agnes screamed out to a
policeman to write to the housekeeper in Cur-
zon Street to inform her that they were all
burnt alive. . . .

SYDNEY SMITH TO LADY HOLLAND.

LONDON, November 6, 1842.

I have not the heart, when an amiable lady
says, "Come to 'Semiramis' in my box," to

decline; but I get bolder at a distance. "Semiramis" would be to me pure misery. I love
music very little—I hate acting; I have the
worst opinion of Semiramis herself, and the
whole thing (I cannot help it) seems so childish
and so foolish that I cannot abide it. Moreover, it would be rather out of etiquette for a
Canon of St. Paul's to go to an opera; and
where etiquette prevents me from doing things
disagreeable to myself, I am a perfect martinet.
All these things considered, I am sure you will
not be a Semiramis to me, but let me off.

———

SYDNEY SMITH TO MRS. APREECE.

HESLINGTON, December 29, 1811.

I am very much flattered by your recollection of me, and by your obliging letter. I have
been following the plough. My talk has been
of oxen, and I have gloried in the goad.

Your letter operated as a charm. I remem-
bered that there were better things than these;
that there was a metropolis; that there were
wits, chemists, poets, splendid feasts, and capti-
vating women. Why remind a Yorkshire resident clergyman of these things, and put him to
recollect human beings at Rome, when he is
fattening beasts at Ephesus? . . . .

I shall be in London in March. Pray remain single, and marry nobody (let him be whom he may): you will be annihilated the moment you do, and, instead of an alkali or an acid, become a neutral salt. You may very likely be happier yourself, but you will be lost to your male friends. . . .

SYDNEY SMITH TO THOMAS MOORE.

June 15, 1831.

By the beard of the Prelate of Canterbury, by the cassock of the Prelate of York, by the breakfasts of Rogers, by Luttrell's love of side-dishes, I swear that I had rather hear you sing than any person I ever heard in my life, male or female. . . . Call me Dissenter, say that my cassock is ill put on, that I know not the delicacies of decimation, and confound the greater and smaller tithes; but do not think or say that I am insensible to your music. . . .

SYDNEY SMITH TO RODERICK I. MURCHISON.

COMBE FLOREY, December 26, 1841.

. . . . There are no people here, and no events, so I have no news to tell you, except that in this mild climate my orange-trees are now out-of-doors and in full bearing. Imme-

diately before my window there are twelve
large oranges on one tree. The trees themselves are not the Linnæan orange-tree, but
what are popularly called the bay-tree, in large
green boxes of the most correct shape, and the
oranges well secured to them with the best
packthread. They are universally admired, and,
upon the whole, considered to be finer than the
Ludovican orange-trees of Versailles.

SYDNEY SMITH TO FRANCIS JEFFREY.

LONDON, 1806.

. . . . Tell Murray that I was much struck
with the politeness of Miss Markham the day
after he went. In carving a partridge, I splashed
her with gravy from head to foot; and though
I saw three distinct brown rills of animal juice
trickling down her cheek, she had the complais-
ance to swear that not a drop had reached her!
Such circumstances are the triumphs of civilized life. . . .

SYDNEY SMITH TO LADY HOLLAND.

COMBE FLOREY, September 29, 1829.

. . . Luttrell came over for a day, from whence
I know not, but I thought not from good pas-
tures; at least, he had not his usual soup-and-

pattie look. There was a forced smile upon his countenance, which seemed to indicate plain roast and boiled, and a sort of apple-pudding depression, as if he had been staying with a clergyman. . . .

SYDNEY SMITH TO N. FAZAKERLY.

COMBE FLOREY, October, 1829.

. . . I was at Bowood last week: the only persons there were sea-shore Calcott and his wife—two very sensible, agreeable people. Luttrell came over for the day; he was very agreeable, but spoke too lightly, I thought, of veal soup. I took him aside, and reasoned the matter with him, but in vain; to speak the truth, Luttrell is not steady in his judgment on dishes. Individual failures with him soon degenerate into generic objections, till, by some fortunate accident, he eats himself into better opinions. A person of more calm reflection thinks not only of what he is consuming at that moment, but of the soups of the same kind he has met with in a long course of dining, and which have gradually and justly elevated the species. I am perhaps making too much of this; but the failures of a man of sense are always painful. . . .

SYDNEY SMITH TO MRS. MEYNELL.

COMBE FLOREY, 1843.

. . . Luttrell is staying here.   Nothing can
exceed the innocence of our conversation.   It is
one continued eulogy upon man-and-woman-
kind.   You would suppose that two Arcadian
old gentlemen, after shearing their flocks, had
agreed to spend a week together upon curds
and cream, and to indulge in gentleness of
speech and softness of mind. . . .

———

SYDNEY SMITH TO LORD MURRAY.

COMBE FLOREY, September 29, 1843.

. . . You are, I hear, attending more to diet
than heretofore.   If you wish for any thing
like happiness in the fifth act of life, eat and
drink about one half what you *could* eat and
drink.   Did I ever tell you my calculation
about eating and drinking?   Having ascertained the weight of what I could live upon, so
as to preserve health and strength, and what I
did live upon, I found that between ten and
seventy years of age I had eaten and drunk
forty-four horse wagon-loads of meat and drink
more than would have preserved me in life and

health! The value of this mass of nourish-
ment I considered to be worth seven thousand
pounds sterling. It occurred to me that I
must, by my voracity, have starved to death
fully a hundred persons. This is a frightful
calculation, but irresistibly true, and I think,
dear Murray, your wagons would require an additional horse each! . . .

CHARLES LAMB TO THOMAS MANNING.

December 25, 1815.

Dear old friend and absentee :—This is
Christmas Day, 1815, with us. What it may
be with you I don't know, the 12th of June
next year perhaps ; and if it should be the con-
secrated season with you, I don't see how you
can keep it. You have no turkeys ; you would
not desecrate the festival by offering up a withered Chinese bantam, instead of the savory
grand Norfolcian holocaust that smokes all
around my nostrils at this moment from a thousand firesides. Then what puddings have you?
where will you get holly to stick in your
churches, or churches to stick your dried tea-
leaves (that must be the substitute) in? What
memorials you can have of the holy time, I

see not. A chopped missionary or two may
keep up the thin idea of Lent and the wilderness; but what standing evidence have you of
the Nativity?—'t is our rosy-cheeked, home-
stalled divines, whose faces shine to the tune of
unto us a child was born; faces fragrant with
the mince-pies of half a century, that alone can
authenticate the cheerful mystery—I feel, I
feel my bowels refreshed with the holy tide—
my zeal is great against the unedified heathen.
Down with the pagodas; down with the idols
—Ching-chong-fo—and his foolish priesthood!
Come out of Babylon, O my friend! for her
time is come, and the child that is native, and
the Proselyte of her gates, shall kindle and
smoke together! And in sober sense what
makes you so long from among us, Manning?
You must not expect to see the same England
again which you left.

Empires have been overturned, crowns trodden into dust, the face of the western world
quite changed: your friends have all got old—
those you left blooming—myself (who am one
of the few that remember you) those golden
hairs which you recollect my taking a pride
in, turned to silvery and gray. . . .

CHARLES LAMB TO SAMUEL TAYLOR COLERIDGE.

March 9, 1822.

It gives me great satisfaction to hear that the pig turned out so well—they are interesting creatures at a certain age—what a pity such buds should blow out into the maturity of rank bacon! You had all some of the crackling— and brain sauce—did you remember to rub it with butter, and gently dredge it a little, just before the crisis? Did the eyes come away kindly with no Œdipean avulsion? Was the crackling the color of the ripe pomegranate? Had you no cursed complement of boiled neck of mutton before it, to blunt the edge of delicate desire? Did you flesh maiden teeth in it? Not that I sent the pig, or can form the remotest guess what part Owen could play in the business. I never knew him give any thing away in my life. He would not begin with strangers. I suspect the pig, after all, was meant for me; but at the unlucky juncture of time being absent, the present somehow went round to Highgate. To confess an honest truth, a pig is one of those things I could never think of sending away. Teals, widgeons, snipes, barn-door fowl, ducks, geese—your tame villatic things—Welsh

mutton, collars of brawn, sturgeon, fresh or
pickled, your potted char, Swiss cheeses, French
pies, early grapes, muscadines, I impart as freely
unto my friends as to myself. They are but
self-extended; but pardon me if I stop somewhere—where the fine feeling of benevolence
giveth a higher smack than the sensual rarity—
there my friends (or any good man) may command me; but pigs are pigs, and I myself
therein am nearest to myself. Nay, I should
think it an affront, an undervaluing done to
Nature who bestowed such a boon upon me, if
in a churlish mood I parted with the precious
gift. One of the bitterest pangs of remorse I
ever felt was when a child—when my kind old
aunt had strained her pocket-strings to bestow
a sixpenny whole plum-cake upon me. In my
way home through the Borough, I met a venerable old man, not a mendicant, but thereabouts
—a look-beggar, not a verbal petitionist; and
in the coxcombry of taught-charity I gave
away the cake to him. I walked on a little in
all the pride of an Evangelical peacock, when
of a sudden my old aunt's kindness crossed me
—the sum it was to her—the pleasure she had
a right to expect that I—not the old impostor

—should take in eating her cake—the cursed
ingratitude by which, under the color of a
Christian virtue, I had frustrated her cherished
purpose. I sobbed, wept, and took it to heart
so grievously, that I think I never suffered the
like—and I was right. It was a piece of unfeeling hypocrisy, and it proved a lesson to me
ever after. . . .

CHARLES LAMB TO THOMAS MANNING.

LONDON, February 24, 1805.

I have been very unwell since I saw you. A
sad depression of spirits, a most unaccountable
nervousness; from which I have been partially
relieved by an odd accident. You knew Dick
Hopkins, the swearing scullion of Caius? This
fellow, by industry and agility, has thrust himself into the important situations (no sinecures,
believe me) of cook to Trinity Hall and Caius
College: and the generous creature has con-
trived with the greatest delicacy imaginable, to
send me a present of Cambridge brawn. What
makes it the more extraordinary is, that the
man never saw me in his life that I know of. I
suppose he has *heard* of me. I did not immediately recognize the donor; but one of Richard's cards, which had accidentally fallen into

the straw, detected him in a moment.   Dick,
you know, was always remarkable for flourishing. His card imports, that "orders (to wit, for
brawn), from any part of England, Scotland, or
Ireland, will be duly executed," etc.   At first,
I thought of declining the present; but Richard knew my blind side when he pitched upon
brawn.   'T is of all my hobbies the supreme in
the eating way.   He might have sent sop from
the pan, skimmings, crumpets, chips, hog's lard,
the tender brown judiciously scalped from a
fillet of veal (dexterously replaced by a sala-
mander), the tops of asparagus, fugitive livers,
runaway gizzards of fowls, the eyes of mar-
tyred pigs, ... the red spawn of lobsters,
leveret's ears, and such pretty filchings common to cooks; but these had been ordinary
presents, the every-day courtesies of dish-
washers to their sweethearts.   Brawn was a
noble thought.   It is not every common gullet-
fanьier that can properly esteem of it.   It is
like a picture by one of the choice old Italian
masters.   Its gusto is of that hidden sort.   As
Wordsworth sings of a modest poet,—" you
must love him, ere to you he will seem worthy
of your love"; so brawn, you must taste it, ere

to you it will seem to have any taste at all. But 't is nuts to the adept : those that will send out their tongues and feelers to find it out.   It will be wooed, and not unsought be won. Now, ham-essence, lobsters, turtle, such popular minions, absolutely *court you*, lay themselves out to strike you at first smack, like one of David's pictures (they call him *Darveed*), compared with the plain russet-coated wealth of a Titian or a Correggio, as I illustrated above. Such are the obvious glaring heathen virtues of a corporation dinner, compared with the reserved collegiate worth of brawn. . . .

CHARLES LAMB TO THOMAS MANNING.

LONDON, August 22, 1800.

You need not imagine any apology necessary. Your fine hare and fine birds (which just now are dangling by our kitchen blaze) discourse most eloquent music in your justification. You just nicked my palate. For, with all due decorum and leave may it be spoken, my worship hath taken physic to-day, and being low and puling, requireth to be pampered. Foh ! how beautiful and strong those buttered onions come to my nose ! For you must know we ex-

tract a divine spirit of gravy from those materials which duly compounded with a consist-
ence of bread and cream (y' clept bread-sauce),
each to each giving double grace, do mutually
illustrate and set off (as skilful goldfoils to rare
jewels) your partridge, pheasant, woodcock,
snipe, teal, widgeon, and the other lesser
daughters of the ark. My friendship, strug-
gling with my carnal and fleshly prudence
(which suggests that a bird a man is the proper
allotment in such cases), yearneth sometimes
to have thee here to pick a wing or so. I question if your Norfolk sauces match our London
culinaric.

George Dyer has introduced me to the table
of an agreeable old gentleman, Dr. Anderson,
who gives hot legs of mutton and grape pies at
his sylvan lodge at Isleworth, where, in the
middle of a street, he has shot up a wall most
preposterously before his small dwelling, which,
with the circumstance of his taking several
panes of glass out of bedroom windows (for
air) causeth his neighbors to speculate strangely on the state of the good man's pericranicks.
Plainly, he lives under the reputation of being
deranged. George does not mind this circum-

stance; he rather likes him the better for it. The Doctor, in his pursuits, joins agricultural to poetical science, and has set George's brains mad about old Scotch writers, Barbour, Douglas's Æneid, Blind Harry, etc. We returned home in a return postchaise (having dined with the Doctor), and George kept wondering and wondering, for eight or nine turnpike miles, what was the name, and striving to recollect the name of a poet anterior to Barbour. I begged to know what was remaining of his works. "There is nothing *extant* of his works, sir, but by all accounts he seems to have been a fine genius!" This fine genius, without anything to show for it or any title beyond George's courtesy, without even a name! and Barbour, and Douglas, and Blind Harry, now are the predominant sounds in George's pia mater, and their buzzings exclude politics, criticism, and algebra—the late lords of that illustrious lumber-room. Mark, he has never read any of these bucks, but is impatient till he reads them *all* at the Doctor's suggestion. Poor Dyer! his friends should be careful what sparks they let fall into such inflammable matter. . . .

God bless me, here are the birds, smoking hot!

Vol. III.

All that is gross and unspiritual in me rises at the sight!

Avaunt friendship and all memory of absent friends!

CHARLES LAMB TO THOMAS MANNING.

LONDON, November, 1802. (?)

. . . I 've often wished I lived in the Golden Age, before doubts and propositions and corollaries got into the world. *Now*, as Joseph Cottle, a bard of nature, sings, going up Malvern Hills,

> " How steep! how painful the ascent!
> It needs the evidence of *close deduction*
> To know that ever I shall gain the top."

You must know that Joe is lame, so that he had some reason for so singing. These two lines, I assure you, are taken *totidem literis* from a very *popular* poem. Joe is also an epic poet as well as a descriptive, and has written a tragedy, though both his drama and epopoiea are strictly *descriptive*, and chiefly of the *beauties of nature*, for Joe thinks *man* with all his passions and frailties not a proper subject of the *drama*. Joe's tragedy hath the following surpassing speech in it. Some king is told that his enemy has engaged twelve archers to come over in a boat from an enemy's country and way-lay him; he thereupon pathetically exclaims:

" *Twelve* dost thou say ? Curse on those dozen villains ! "

Cottle read two or three acts out to us, very gravely on both sides, till he came to this heroic touch,—and then he asked what we laughed at. I had no more muscles that day. A poet that chooses to read out his own verses has but a limited power over you.* There is a bound where his authority ceases. . . .

CHARLES LAMB TO SAMUEL TAYLOR COLERIDGE.

LONDON, April 13, 1803.

. . . What do you think of smoking ? I want your sober *average noon opinion* of it. I generally am eating my dinner about the time I should determine it.

* An instance of quite unlimited power and boundless authority on the part of a reader is given by Moore in his "Diary" (July, 1819): " George Dyer, in despair of getting any one to listen to him reading his own poetry, at last, when Dr. Graham came into the neighborhood with his plan of burying people up to the neck in the earth and leaving them there some hours (as a mode of cure for some disease), took advantage of the situation of these patients, and read to them all while they were thus stuck in the earth ! "

Morning is a girl and can't smoke—she 's no evidence one way or the other; and Night is so evidently *bought over* that he can't be a very upright judge. May be the truth is that *one* pipe is wholesome, *two* pipes toothsome, *three* pipes noisome, *four* pipes fulsome, *five* pipes quarrelsome, and that 's the *sum* on 't. But that is deciding rather upon rhyme than reason. . . . After all, our instincts *may* be best. Wine, I am sure,—good, mellow, generous port,—can hurt nobody, unless those who take it to excess, which they may easily avoid if they observe the rules of temperance.

Bless you, old sophist, who next to human nature taught me all the corruption I was capable of knowing ! . . .

CHARLES LAMB TO SAMUEL TAYLOR COLERIDGE.

LONDON, June 7, 1809.

. . . Clarkson tells me you are in a smoky house. Have you cured it ? It is hard to cure any thing of smoking. Our little poems are but humble, but they have no name.* You must read them, remembering they were task-work, and perhaps you will admire the number

* " Poetry for Children," published anonymously in 1809.

of subjects, all of children, picked out by an old bachelor and an old maid. Many parents would not have found so many. Have you read "Cœlebs"? It has reached eight editions in so many weeks; yet literally it is one of the very poorest sort of common novels, with the drawback of dull religion in it. Had the religion been high and flavored, it would have been something. I borrowed this "Cœlebs in Search of a Wife" of a very careful, neat lady, and returned it with this stuff written in the beginning:

> " If ever I marry a wife
>   I 'd marry a landlord's daughter,
>   For then I may sit in the bar,
>   And drink cold brandy-and-water."

CHARLES LAMB TO BASIL MONTAGU.

WINTERSLOW, NEAR SARUM, July 12, 1810.

. . . We purpose setting out for Oxford Tuesday fortnight, and coming thereby home. But no more night travelling. My head is sore (understand it of the inside) with that deduction of my natural rest which I suffered coming down. Neither Mary nor I can spare a morsel of our rest: it is incumbent on us to be misers of it. Travelling is not good for us—we

travel so seldom.   If the sun be hell, it is not
for the fire, but for the sempiternal motion of
that miserable Body of Light.   How much more
dignified leisure hath a mussel glued to his un-
passable rocky limit, two inch square !   He
hears the tide roll over him, backwards and
forwards twice a day (as the damn'd Salisbury
Long Coach goes and returns in eight-and-forty
hours), but knows better than to take an outside night-place a top on 't.   He is the owl of
the sea—Minerva's fish—the fish of wisdom. . . .

CHARLES LAMB TO BERNARD BARTON.

January 9, 1824.

DEAR B. B. :—Do you know what it is to
succumb under an insurmountable day-mare,—
" a whoreson lethargy," Falstaff calls it,—an
indisposition to do any thing, or to be any
thing ; a total deadness and distaste ; a suspension of vitality ; an indifference to locality ; a
numb, soporifical, good-for-nothingness ; an os-
sification all over ; an oyster-like insensibility
to the passing events ; a mind-stupor ; a brawny
defiance to the needles of a thrusting-in conscience ?   Did you ever have a very bad cold,
with a total irresolution to submit to water-

gruel processes? This has been for many weeks my lot, and my excuse ; my fingers drag heavily over this paper, and to my thinking, it is three-and-twenty furlongs from here to the end of this demi-sheet. I have not a thing to say; nothing is of more importance than another; I am flatter than a denial or a pancake; emptier than Judge ———'s wig when the head is in it ; duller than a country stage when the actors are off it ; a cipher, an O! I acknowledge life at all only by an occasional convulsional cough, and a permanent phlegmatic pain in the chest. I am weary of the world ; life is weary of me. My day is gone into twilight, and I don't think it worth the expense of candles. My wick hath a thief in it, but I can't muster courage to snuff it. I inhale suffocation ; I can't distinguish veal from mutton; nothing interests me. 'T is twelve o'clock and Thurtell is just now coming out upon the New Drop, Jack Ketch alertly tucking up his greasy sleeves to do the last office of mortality, yet cannot I elicit a groan or a moral reflection. If you told me the world will be at an end tomorrow, I should just say: "Will it?" I have not volition enough left to dot my i's, much

less to comb my eyebrows ; my eyes are set in
my head ; my brains are gone out to see a
poor relation in Moorfields, and they did not
say when they 'd come back again ; my skull is
a Grub Street attic to let,—not so much as a
joint-stool or a crack'd jordan left in it ; my
hand writes, not I, from habit, as chickens run
about a little when their heads are off. O for
a vigorous fit of gout, colic, toothache,—an ear-
wig in my auditory, a fly in my visual organs.
Pain is life,—the sharper the more evidence of
life ; but this apathy, this death ! Did you
ever have an obstinate cold,—a six or seven
weeks' unintermitting chill and suspension of
hope, fear, conscience, and every thing? Yet
do I try all I can to cure it ; I try wine and
spirits, and smoking, and snuff in unsparing
quantities; but they all only seem to make me
worse instead of better. I sleep in a damp
room, but it does me no good ; I come home
late o' nights, but do not find any visible amend-
ment ! Who shall deliver me from the body of
this death ? It is just fifteen minutes after
twelve ; Thurtell is by this time a good way on
his journey, baiting at Scorpion, perhaps !
Ketch is bargaining for his cast-coat and waist-

coat ; the Jew demurs at first at three half-crowns, but on consideration that he may get somewhat by showing them in the town, finally closes.

_____

CHARLES LAMB TO BERNARD BARTON.

May 16, 1826.

. . . I have had my head and ears stuffed up with the east winds. A continual ringing in my brain of bells jangled, or the spheres touched by some raw angel. It is not George the Third trying the Hundredth Psalm? I get my music for nothing. But the weather seems to be softening, and will thaw my stun-nings. Coleridge, writing to me a week or two since, begins his note : " Summer has set in with its usual severity." A cold summer is all I know of disagreeable in cold. I do not mind the utmost rigor of real winter, but these smiling hypocrites of Mays wither me to death. My head has been a ringing chaos, like the day the winds were made, before they submitted to the discipline of a weather-cock,—before the quarters were made. In the street, with the blended noises of life about me, I hear, and my head is lightened ; but in a room the hubbub comes back, and

I am deaf as a sinner. Did I tell you of a pleasant sketch Hood has done, which he calls: "*Very Deaf Indeed*"? It is of a good-natured, stupid-looking old gentleman, whom a footpad has stopped, but for his extreme deafness cannot make him understand what he wants. The unconscious old gentleman is extending his ear-trumpet very complacently, and the fellow is firing a pistol into it to make him hear, but the ball will pierce his skull sooner than the report reach his sensorium. I choose a very little bit of paper, for my ear hisses when I bend down to write. I can hardly read a book, for I miss that small, soft voice which the idea of articulated words raises (almost imperceptibly to you) in a silent reader. I seem too deaf to see what I read. But with a touch or two of returning zephyr my head will melt. What lies you poets tell about the May! It is the most ungenial part of the year. Cold crocuses, cold primroses, you take your blossoms in ice,—a painted sun. . . .

CHARLES LAMB TO ROBERT SOUTHEY.

November 28, 1798.

. . . My tailor has brought me home a new coat, lapelled with a velvet collar. He assures me everybody wears velvet collars now. Some are born fashionable, some achieve fashion, and others, like your humble servant, have fashion thrust upon them. The rogue has been making inroads hitherto by modest degrees, foisting upon me an additional button, recommending gaiters; but to come upon me thus in a full tide of luxury, neither becomes him as a tailor nor the ninth of a man. My meek gentleman was robbed the other day, coming with his wife and family in a one-horse shay from Hampstead; the villains rifled him of four guineas, some shillings and half-pence, and a bundle of customers' measures, which they swore were bank-notes. They did not shoot him, and when they rode off he addrest them with profound gratitude, making a congee: "Gentlemen, I wish you good-night, and we are very much obliged to you that you have not used us ill!" And this is the cuckoo that has had the audacity to foist upon me ten buttons on a side and a black velvet collar. A cursed ninth of a scoundrel! . . .

CHARLES LAMB TO THOMAS MANNING.

LONDON, March 28, 1809.

. . . While I think on it, let me tell you we are moved. Don't come any more to Mitre

Court Buildings. We are at 34 Southampton
Buildings, Chancery Lane, and shall be here till
about the end of May; then we remove to No.
4 Inner Temple Lane, where I mean to live
and die, for I have such horror of moving that
I would not take a benefice from the king, if I
was not indulged with non-residence. What a
dislocation of comfort is comprised in that word
moving! Such a heap of little nasty things,
after you think all is got into the cart; old
dredging-boxes, worn-out brushes, gallipots,
vials, things that it is impossible the most ne-
cessitous person can ever want, but which the
women, who preside on these occasions, will
not leave behind if it was to save your soul;
they'd keep the cart ten minutes to stow in
dirty pipes and broken matches, to show their
economy. Then you can find nothing you
want for many days after you get into your new
lodgings. You must comb your hair with your
fingers, wash your hands without soap, go
about in dirty gaiters. Was I Diogenes, I
would not move out of a kilderkin into a hogs-
head, though the first had had nothing but
small beer in it, and the second reeked claret.
Our place of final destination,—I don't mean

the grave, but No. 4 Inner Temple Lane,—
looks out upon a gloomy churchyard-like court,
called Hare Court, with three trees and a pump
in it. Do you know it? I was born near it,
and used to drink at that pump when I was a
Rechabite of six years old. . . .

CHARLES LAMB TO WALTER SAVAGE LANDOR.

April 9, 1832.

. . . I forgot to tell you that I knew all your
Welch annoyancers, the measureless Bethams,
I knew a quarter of a mile of them.   Seventeen
brothers and sixteen sisters, as they appear to
me in memory.   There was one of them that
used to fix his long legs on my fender, and tell
a tale of a shark every night, endless, immortal.   How have I grudged the salt sea ravener
not having had his gorge of him !   The short-
est of the daughters measured five feet eleven
without her shoes.   Well, some day we may
confer about them.   But they were tall.   Truly
I have discover'd the longitude. . . .

MISCELLANEOUS.

ROBERT SOUTHEY TO THOMAS SOUTHEY.

KESWICK, August 16, 1808.

. . . You will not, perhaps, be surprised to hear that two of my old dreams are likely to be introduced, with powerful effect, in this poem, —good proof that it is worth while to keep even the imperfect register that I have. The fear is that what happened to Nebuchadnezzar is perpetually happening to me. I forget my dreams, and have no Daniel to help out my recollection; and if by chance I do remember them, unless they are instantly written down, the impression passes away almost as lightly as the dream itself. Do you remember the story of Mickle the poet, who always regretted that he could not remember the poetry which he composed in his sleep? It was, he said, so infinitely superior to any thing which he produced in his waking hours. One morning he awoke and repeated the lamentation over his unhappy fortune, that he should compose such sublime poetry and yet lose it forever! "What!" said his wife, who happened to be awake, " were you writing poetry?" "Yes," he replied, "and such poetry that I would give the world to remember it." "Well, then," said she, "I did luckily hear the last lines, and I am sure I remember them exactly, they were:

> " By Heaven I 'll wreak my woes
> Upon the cowslip and the pale primrose."

This is one of Sharpe's stories: it is true, and an excellently good one it is. I am not such a dreamer as Mickle, for what I can remember is worth remembering, and one of the wildest scenes in "Kehama" will prove this. God bless you!

—

THOMAS CARLYLE TO HIS MOTHER.

CHELSEA, February 18, 1841.

I had been summoned again under unheard-of penalties to attend a jury trial about Patent India-rubber Cotton-cards. . . . We sat for two endless days till dark night each day. About eight o'clock at night on the second day we imagined it was done, and we had only to speak our verdict. But, lo and behold! one of the jury stood out. We were eleven for the plaintiff, and one the other way who would not

yield.   The judge told us we must withdraw,
through passages and stairs, up and down into
a little stone cell with twelve old chairs in it,
one candle, and no meat, drink, or fire.   Conceive our humor.   Not a particle of dinner,
nerves worn out, etc.   The refractory man—a
thick-set, flat-headed *sack*—erected himself in
his chair, and said :   " I am one of the firmest-
minded men in England.   I know this room
pretty well.   I have starved out three juries
here already."   Reasoning, demonstration, was
of no avail at all.   They began to suspect he
had been bribed.   He looked really at one time
as if he would keep us till half-past nine in the
morning, and then get us dismissed, the whole
trial to begin *again*.   One really could not help
laughing, though one had a notion to kill the
beast.   " Do not argue with him," I said.
" Flatter him.   Don't you see he has the ob-
stinacy of a boar, and little more sense in that
head of his than in a Swedish turnip ? "   It was
a head all cheeks, jaw, and no brow, of shape
somewhat like a great ball of putty dropped
from a height.   I set to work upon him ; we
all set to work, and in about an hour after our
"withdrawal," the *Hash*, I pulling him by the

arm, was got stirred from his chair—one of the
gladdest moments I had seen for a month—
and in a few instants more we were all rejoicing
on our road home. In my life I have seen
nothing more absurd. . . .

CHARLES MATHEWS TO MRS. MATHEWS.

EDINBURGH, February 9, 1822.

I know too many people here to study undisturbed; therefore am obliged to hide myself
in the private walks, when the weather will permit. Yesterday was lovely, and I had a good
spell; to-day boisterous and wet. Terry declared that he was blown off the pavement into
the middle of the street, from the violence of a
squall, and must have fallen, if he had not made
a snatch at a man who returned his hug, like
two people on the ice. I have had two nights,
the first £80, for they would not be persuaded
that I was myself, in consequence of the dis-
turbance Irish Mathews occasioned here. But
believing from ocular demonstration that I *was*
I, my second amounted to £132, which, to ap-
preciate, you must be acquainted with circumstances too tedious, etc. When I tell you that
the boxes will only hold £55, you may suppose

what it was. Sir Walter, the magician of the
North, and all his family, were there. They
huzzaed when he came in, and I *never* played
with such spirit, I was so proud of his presence.
Coming out, I saw him in the lobby, and very
quietly shook his hand. " How d' ye do, Sir
Walter? "—" Oh, hoo *are* ye? wall, hoo have
you been entertained?" (I perceived he did
not know me.)—" Why, sir, I don't think quite
so well as the rest of the people."—" Why not?
I have been *just* delighted.   It 's quite wonderful hoo the devil he gets through it all."—
(Whispering in his ear) :   " I am surprised too;
but I did it all myself."   Lockhart, Lady
Scott, and the children quickly perceived the
equivoque, and laughed aloud, which drew all
eyes upon me; an invitation for to-morrow
followed, which I accepted joyfully.   I doubt
if the players in Shakespeare's time appreciated
his invite as I do an attention from the man
who in my mind is second only to him.

———

SIR WALTER SCOTT TO ——

ABBOTSFORD, October 30, 1828.

. . . I cannot help adding . . . a sporting
anecdote, said to have happened in Fife, . . .

which may serve to show in what regard the
rules of fair play between hound and hare are
held by Scottish sportsmen. There was a
coursing club, once upon a time, which met at
Balchristy, in the Province, or, as it is popularly
called, the Kingdom of Fife. The members
were elderly, social men, whom a very moderate
allowance of sport served as an introduction to
a hearty dinner and jolly evening. Now, there
had her seat on the ground where they usually
met, a certain large stout hare, who seemed
made on purpose to entertain these moderate
sportsmen. She usually gave the amusement
of three or four turns, as soon as she was put
up,—a sure sign of a strong hare, when prac-
tised by any beyond the age of a leveret,—
then stretched out in great style, and after af-
fording the gentlemen an easy canter of a mile
or two, threw out the dogs, by passing through
a particular gap in an inclosure. This sport the
same hare gave to the same party for one or
two seasons, and it was just enough to afford
the worthy members of the club a sufficient
reason to be alleged to their wives, or others
whom it may concern, for passing the day in
the public-house. At length, a fellow who at-

tended the hunt nefariously, thrust his plaid, or great coat, into the gap I mentioned, and poor puss, her retreat being thus cut off, was, in the language of the dying Desdemona, " basely—basely murdered." The sport of the Balchristy club seemed to end with this famous hare. They either found no hares, or such as afforded only a halloo and a squeak, or such, finally, as gave them farther runs than they had pleasure of following. The spirit of the meeting died away, and at length it was altogether given up.

The publican was, of course, the party most especially affected by the discontinuance of the club, and regarded, it may be supposed, with no complacency, the person who had prevented the hare from escaping, and even his memory. One day, a gentleman asked him what was become of such a one, naming the obnoxious individual. " He is dead, sir," answered mine host, with an angry scowl, " and his soul kens this day whether the hare of Balchristy got fair play or not."

CHARLES DICKENS TO DOUGLAS JERROLD.

PARIS, February 14, 1847.

. . . I am somehow reminded of a good story I heard the other night from a man who was a witness of it, and an actor in it. At a certain German town last autumn there was a tremendous *furore* about Jenny Lind, who, after driving the whole place mad, left it, on her travels, early one morning. The moment her carriage was outside the gates a party of rampant students, who had escorted it, rushed back to the inn, demanded to be shown to her bedroom, swept like a whirlwind up-stairs into the room indicated to them, tore up the sheets and wore them in strips as decorations. An hour or two afterwards a bald old gentleman of amiable appearance, an Englishman, who was staying in the hotel, came to breakfast at the *table d'hôte*, and was observed to be much disturbed in his mind, and to show great terror whenever a student came near him. At last he said, in a low voice, to some people who were near him at the table : " You are English gentlemen, I observe. Most extraordinary people these Germans! Students, as a body, raving mad, gentlemen!" " O, no!" said somebody else ; " excitable, but very good fellows, and very sensible." " By God, sir," returned the old gentleman, still more disturbed; "then there is something political in it, and I am a marked man. I went out for a little walk this morning after shaving, and while I was gone "—he fell into a terrible perspiration as he told it—"they burst into my bedroom, tore up my sheets, and are now patrolling the town in all directions with bits of 'em in their button-holes!" I need n't wind up by adding that they had gone to the wrong chamber. . . .

MRS. ANNE GRANT TO MRS. SMITH.

EDINBURGH, December 10, 1816.

. . . A young lady from England, very ambitious of distinction, and thinking the outrageous admiration of genius was nearly as good as the possession of it, was presented to Walter Scott, and had very nearly gone through the regular forms of swooning sensibility on the occasion. Being afterwards introduced to Mr. Henry Mackenzie, she bore it better, but kissed his hand with admiring veneration. It is worth telling, for the sake of Mr. Scott's comment. He said: "Did you ever hear the like of that English lass, to faint at the sight of a cripple Clerk of Session, and kiss the dry, withered hand of an old tax-gatherer?" . . .

MISS MARY LAMB TO MISS SARAH STODDART.

September, 1805.

Certainly you are the best letter-writer (besides being the best hand) in the world. I

have just been reading over again your two
long letters, and I perceive they make me very
envious. I have taken a brand new pen, and
put on my *spectacles*, and am peering with all
my might to see the lines in the paper, which
the sight of your even lines had well nigh
tempted me to rule ; and I have, moreover,
taken two pinches of snuff extraordinary, to
clear my head, which feels more cloudy than
common this fine, cheerful morning. . . .
Your brother gave me most unlimited orders
to domineer over you, to be the inspector of
all your actions, and to direct and govern
you with a stern voice and a high hand, to
be, in short, a very elder brother over you,—
does not the hearing of this, my meek pupil,
make you long to come to London? I am
making all the proper inquiries against the
time of the newest and most approved modes
(being myself mainly ignorant in these points)
of etiquette, and nicely corrected maidenly
manners.

But to speak seriously. I mean, when we
meet, that we will lay our heads together, and
consult and contrive the best way of making
the best girl in the world the fine lady her

brother wishes to see her; and believe me,
Sarah, it is not so difficult a matter as one is
sometimes apt to imagine. I have observed
many a demure lady, who passes muster ad-
mirably well, who, I think, we could easily
learn to imitate in a week or two. We will
talk of these things when we meet. . . .

CHARLES LAMB TO BERNARD BARTON.

November 22, 1823.

. . . You are too much apprehensive of your
complaint; I know many that are always ail-
ing of it, and live on to a good old age. I
know a merry fellow (you partly know him)
who, when his medical adviser told him he had
drunk away all *that part*, congratulated himself
(now his liver was gone) that he should be the
longest liver of the two.

The best way in these cases is to keep yourself as ignorant as you can, as ignorant as the
world was before Galen, of the entire inner
construction of the animal man; not to be conscious of a midriff; to hold kidneys (save of
sheep and swine) to be an agreeable fiction;
not to know whereabouts the gall grows; to
account the circulation of the blood an idle

whimsey of Harvey's to acknowledge no mechanism not visible. For, once fix the seat of your disorder, and your fancies flux into it like bad humors. Those medical gentries choose each his favorite part ; one takes the lungs, another the aforesaid liver, and refer to that, whatever in the animal economy is amiss. Above all, use exercise, take a little more spirituous liquors, learn to smoke, continue to keep a good conscience, and avoid tampering with hard terms of art,—viscosity, scirrhosity, and those bugbears by which simple patients are scared into their graves. Believe the general sense of the mercantile world, which holds that desks are not deadly. It is the mind, good B. B., and not the limbs, that taints by long sitting. Think of the patience of tailors, think how long the Lord Chancellor sits, think of the brooding hen ! . . .

BERNARD BARTON TO MR. CLEMISHA.

WOODBRIDGE, December 16, 1843.

I am not a little diverted by thy *taking-on* somewhat about the irksome monotony and confinement of a fortnight's spell at the desk and figure-work, and seeming to thyself like a piece of machinery in consequence. I have really been so unfeeling as to have a hearty laugh about the whole affair. Why, man! I took my seat on the identical stool I now occupy at the desk, to the wood of which I have now well nigh grown, in the third month of the year 1810; and there I have sat on for three and thirty blessed years, beside the odd eight months, without one month's respite in all that time. I believe I once had a fortnight; and once in about two years, or better, I get a week; but all of my absences put together would not make up the eight odd months. I often wonder that my health has stood this sedentary probation as it has, and that my mental faculties have survived three and thirty years of putting down figures in three rows, casting them up, and carrying them forward *ad infinitum.* Nor is this all—for during that time, I think, I have put forth some half dozen volumes of verse, to say nothing of scores and scores of odd bits of verse contributed to annuals, periodicals, albums, and what not; and a correspondence implying a hundred times the *writing* of all these put together; where is the wonder that on the verge of sixty

I am somewhat of a prematurely old man, with
odds and ends of infirmities and ailments about
me, which at times are a trial to the spirits and
a weariness to the flesh ? But all the grumbling
in the world would not mend the matter, or
help me, so I rub and drive on as well as I can.

DAVID GARRICK TO WILLIAM POWELL.

PARIS, December 12, 1764.

Though I have neglected to answer your
obliging letter, I am sure your good-nature
readily excused me, when you heard how unfit
I have lately been to pay my debt of friendship in that way; the writing a letter has, till
within this fortnight, been a labor to me, and
which I should have undergone with pleasure,
could I have been of the least service to you.
The news of your great success gave me a most
sensible pleasure,—the continuance of that success will be in your own power; and if you will
give an older soldier leave to hint a little ad-
vice to you, I will answer for its being sincere
at least, which, from a brother actor, is no small
merit. The gratitude you have expressed for
what little service I did you the summer before
your appearance upon the stage, has attached

me to you, as a man who shall always have my best wishes for his welfare, and my best endeavors to promote it. I have not always met with gratitude in a playhouse. You have acted a greater variety of characters than I could expect in the first winter, and I have some fears that your good-nature to your brother actors (which is commendable when it is not injurious) drove you into parts too precipitately; however, you succeeded, and it is happy that you had the whole summer to correct the errors of haste, which the public will ever excuse in a young performer, on account of his beauties; but now is the time to make sure of your ground in every step you take. You must, therefore, give to study, and an accurate consideration of your characters, those hours which young men too generally give to their friends and flatterers. The common excuse is, "they frequent clubs for the sake of their benefit"; but nothing can be more absurd or contemptible,—your benefits will only increase with your fame, and should that ever sink by your idleness, those friends who have made you idle will be the first to forsake you. When the public has marked you for a favorite (and their

favor must be purchased with sweat and labor),
you may choose what company you please, and
none but the best can be of service to you.

The famous *Baron* of France used to say
that an actor should be "nursed in the lap of
queens"; by which he meant that the best
accomplishments were necessary to form a great
actor. Study hard, my friend, for seven years,
and you may play the rest of your life. I
would advise you to read at your leisure other
books besides plays in which you are concerned.
Our friend Colman will direct you in these matters, and as he loves, and is a good judge of
acting, consult him as often as you can upon
your theatrical affairs. But above all, never let
your *Shakespeare* be out of your hands, or
your pocket; keep him about you as a charm;
the more you read him the more you will like
him, and the better you will act him. One thing
more, and then I will finish my preaching:
guard against *the splitting the ears of the ground-
lings, who are capable of nothing but dumb show
and noise*—do not sacrifice your taste and feelings to the applause of the multitude; a true
genius will convert an audience to his manner,
rather than be converted by them to what is

false and unnatural;—*be not too tame neither.*
I shall leave the rest to the friendship of Colman and your own genius. . . .

MRS. CATHERINE CLIVE TO DAVID GARRICK.

TWICKENHAM, January 23, 1776.

Is it really true that you have put an end to
the glory of Drury Lane Theatre? *If it is so,*
let me congratulate my dear Mr. and Mrs. Garrick on their approaching happiness; *I know*
what it will be; you cannot yet have an idea
of it; *but* if you should still be so wicked not
to be satisfied with that *unbounded,* uncommon
degree of fame you have received as an actor,
and which no other actor ever did receive—nor
no other actor ever can receive :—I say, if you
should still long to be dipping your fingers in
their theatrical pudding (now without plums),
you will be no Garrick for the Pivy.*

In the height of the public admiration for
you, when you were never mentioned with any
other appellation but the Garrick, the charming
man, the fine fellow, the delightful creature,
both by men and ladies; when they were admiring every thing you did, and every thing

* A pet name which Garrick used to call her—" Clivy-pivy."

you scribbled, at this very time, *I, the Pivy,*
was a living witness that they did not know,
nor could they be sensible of, half your perfec-
tions. I have seen you, with your magical
hammer in your hand, *endeavoring* to beat your
ideas into the heads of creatures who had none
of their own ; I have seen you, with lamb-like
patience, endeavoring to make them compre-
hend you ; and I have seen you when that
could not be done ; I have seen your lamb
turned into a lion—by this your great labor and
pains the public was entertained—; *they* thought
they all acted very fine ; they did not see you
pull the wires.

There are people *now* on the stage to whom
you gave their consequence ; they think themselves very great ; now let them go on in their
new parts without your leading-strings, and
they will soon convince the world what their
genius is ; I have always said this to everybody,
even when your horses and mine were in their
highest prancing. While I was under your
control I did not say half the fine things I
thought of you, because it looked like flattery ;
and you know your Pivy was always proud ;
besides, I thought you did not like me then ;

but *now* I am sure you do, which makes me send you this letter. . . .

———

MISS HANNAH MORE TO DAVID GARRICK.

Bristol, June 10, 1776.

I have devoured the newspapers for the last week with the appetite of a famished politician, to learn if my general had yet laid down arms ; but I find you go on with a true American spirit, destroying thousands of his Majesty's liege subjects, breaking the limbs of many, and the hearts of all. . . .

I think by the time this reaches you I may congratulate you on the end of your labors, and the completion of your fame—a fame which has had no parallel, and will have no end.　Yet, whatever reputation the world may ascribe to you, I, who have had the happy privilege of knowing you intimately, shall always think you derived your greatest glory from the temperance with which you enjoyed it, and the true greatness of mind with which you laid it down.　Surely to have suppressed your talents in the moment of your highest capacity for exerting them, does as much honor to your heart as the exertion itself did to your

dramatic character; but I cannot trust myself
on this subject, because, as Sterne says, I am
writing to the man himself; yet I ought to be
indulged,—for, is not the recollection of my
pleasures all that is left me of them? Have I
not seen in one season that *man* act *seven*-and-
twenty times, and rise each time in excellence,
and shall I be silent? Have I not spent three
months under the roof of that man and his
dear charming lady, and received from them
favors that would take me another three months
to tell over, and shall I be silent?

But highly as I enjoy your glory (for I do
enjoy it most heartily, and seem to partake it
too, as I think a ray of it falls on all your
friends), yet I tremble for your health. It is
impossible you can do so much mischief to the
nerves of other people without hurting your
own—in "Richard" especially, where your
murders are by no means confined to the
Tower; but you assassinate your whole audience who have hearts; I say I tremble, lest you
should suffer for all this; but it is over now,
as I hope are the bad effects of it to yourself.
You may break your *wand* at the end of your
trial, when you lay down the office of *haut in-*

tendant of the passions; but the enchantment it raised you can never break, while the memories and feelings remain of those who were ever admitted into the magic circle. . . .

CHARLES DICKENS TO MARK LEMON.

PARIS, Monday, January 7, 1856.

. . . In a piece at the Ambigu, called the "Rentrée à Paris," a mere scene in honor of the return of the troops from the Crimea the other day, there is a novelty which I think it worth letting you know of, as it is easily available, either for a serious or a comic interest— the introduction of a supposed electric telegraph. The scene is the railway terminus at Paris, with the electric telegraph-office on the prompt side, and the clerks *with their backs to the audience*—much more real than if they were, as they infallibly would be, staring about the house—working the needles; and the little bell perpetually ringing. There are assembled to greet the soldiers all the easily and naturally imagined elements of interest—old veteran fathers, young children, agonized mothers, sisters and brothers, girl lovers—each impatient to know of his or her own object of solicitude.

Enter to these a certain marquis, full of sympathy for all, who says " My friends, I am one of you. My brother has no commission yet. He is a common soldier. I wait for him as well as all brothers and sisters here wait for *their* brothers. Tell me whom you are expecting." Then they all tell him. Then he goes into the telegraph-office, and sends a message down the line to know how long the troops will be. Bell rings. Answer handed out on a slip of paper. " Delay on the line. Troops will not arrive for a quarter of an hour." General disappointment. " But we have this brave electric telegraph, my friends," says the marquis. " Give me your little messages, and I 'll send them off." General rush round the marquis. Exclamations: " How 's Henri?" "My love to Georges." " Has Guillaume forgotten Elise?" " Is my son wounded?" " Is my brother promoted?" etc., etc. Marquis composes tumult. Sends message—such a regiment, such a company, " Elise's love to Georges." Little bell rings, slip of paper handed out—" Georges in ten minutes will embrace his Elise. Sends her a thousand kisses." Marquis sends message—such a regiment, such a company—" Is my son wounded ? " Little bell rings. Slip of paper handed out—" No. He has not yet upon him those marks of bravery in the glorious service of his country which his dear old father bears " (father being lamed and invalided). Last of all, the widowed mother. Marquis sends message—such a regiment, such a company—" Is my only son safe ? " Little bell rings. Slip of paper handed out—" He was first upon the heights of Alma." General cheer. Bell rings again, another slip of paper handed out—" He was made a sergeant at Inkermann." Another cheer. Bell rings again, another slip of paper handed out—" He was made color-sergeant at Sebastopol." Another cheer. Bell rings again, another slip of paper handed out—" He was the first man who leaped with the French banner on the Malakhoff tower." Tremendous cheer. Bell rings again, another slip of paper handed out—" But he was struck down there by a musket-ball, and—troops have proceeded. Will arrive in half a minute after this." Mother abandons all hope ; general commiseration ; troops rush in, down a platform ; son only wounded, and embraces her.

As I have said, and as you will see, this is
available for any purpose. But done with equal
distinction and rapidity, it is a tremendous effect, and got by the simplest means in the world.
There is nothing in the piece, but it was impossible not to be moved and excited by the
telegraph part of it. . . .

MRS. THOMAS CARLYLE TO HER HUSBAND.

RAMSGATE, August 5, 1861.

Very charming does n't that look, with the
sea in front as far as eye can reach?* And
that seen (the East Cliff), you need n't wish to
ever see more of Ramsgate. It is made up of
narrow, steep, confused streets like the worst
parts of Brighton. The shops look nasty, the
people nasty, the smells are nasty! (spoiled
shrimps complicated with cesspool!) Only the
East Cliff is clean, and genteel, and airy; and
would be perfect as sea-quarters if it were n't
for the noise! which is so extraordinary as to
be almost laughable.

Along that still-looking road or street between the houses and gardens are passing and
repassing, from early morning to late night,

* Written on Ramsgate note-paper, with a print of the
harbor, etc.

cries of prawns, shrimps, lollipops,—things one
never wanted, and will never want, of the most
miscellaneous sort; and if that were all! But
a brass band plays all through our breakfast,
and repeats the performance often during the
day, and the brass band is succeeded by a band
of Ethiopians, and that again by a band of female fiddlers! and interspersed with these are
individual barrel-organs, individual Scotch bag-
pipes, individual French horns! Oh, it is
"most expensive!" And the night noises
were not to be estimated by the first night!
These are so many and frequent as to form a
sort of mass of voice; perhaps easier to get
some sleep through than an individual nuis-
ance of cock or dog. There are hundreds of
cocks! and they get waked up at, say, one in
the morning by some outburst of drunken
song or of cat-wailing! and never go to sleep
again (these cocks) but for minutes! and there
are three steeple clocks that strike in succession, and there are doors and gates that slam,
and dogs that bark occasionally, and a saw-
mill, and a mews, etc.,—in short, every thing
you could wish not to hear! And I hear it
all, and am getting to sleep in hearing it! the

bed is so soft and clean, and the room so airy; and then I think under every shock, so triumphantly: "Crow away," "roar away," "bark away," "slam away; you can't disturb Mr. C. at Cheyne Row, that can't you!" and the thought is so soothing, I go off asleep,—till next thing! I might try Geraldine's room; but she has now got an adjoining baby! Yesterday we drove to Broadstairs,—a quieter place, but we saw no lodgings that were likely to be quiet, except one villa at six guineas a week, already occupied.

I sleep about, in intervals of the bands, on sofas during the day. . . .

MRS. RICHARD TRENCH TO HER SON.

RICHMOND, July, 1824.

We came to Richmond this morning, as it was absolutely necessary to change the scene for a few hours after my separation from you. "Perhaps the lady will like to see the steamboat?" cries a dapper waiter, with an air of importance at having so charming a spectacle to offer. In spite of the glare and intense heat, I lifted up my eyes to view what to me was quite new, and saw nothing but long,

snaky trails of smoke, puffing, puffing on towards the right in the direction of the river, and
dishonoring the blue sky and beautiful face of
the Thames.   Then appeared a flaring scarlet
flag ; and lastly, to the tune of " Paddy O'Rafferty," a great green and yellow beetle floating
on its back, with a tall chimney-funnel rising
from its middle, breathing out volumes of
smoke.   This creature swarmed with people.
They were like ants which you could gather
from an ant-hill in a teaspoon, all fervid, and
gaudy, and noisy, and bustling, and important,
and delighted with their truly infernal ma-
chine, only fit for sailing on the Styx ; which
has excluded from the water all beauty and
freshness and variety, and hope, and fear, and
anxiety for friends, and good wishes for a fair
wind.   I wrote for an hour, and asked if the
horrible vision was gone.   " No, ma'am," answered the waiter, triumphantly ; " it 's filling."
I looked up ; there was scarce standing-room ;
the chattering increased ; the sweet strain of
" Paddy O'Rafferty " recommenced.   Smoke
now arose from various places, about, above,
and underneath.   " All 's well," cried a pert,
sharp voice, not in the deep tone of an " An-

cient Mariner," but in that of an ostler of the
high road. The huge dragon of the waters
splashed with its horrid fins, bustled and por-
poised about, slowly and with difficulty worked
itself round, and at last took itself away, passengers and all enveloped in one mantle of
smoke.

" Hence, hence, thou horrid bark, the uncouth child
  Of Commerce and of Coal ! "

DAVID GARRICK TO THOMAS AUGUSTINE ARNE.

I have read your play and rode your horse,
and do not approve of either. They both
want the particular spirit which alone can give
pleasure to the reader and the rider. When
the one wants wit, and the other the spur, they
jog on very heavily. I must keep the horse,
but I have returned you the play. I pretend
to some little knowledge of the last ; but as I
am no jockey, they cannot say that the knowing one is taken in. I am, dear sir, your most
obedient servant.

LORD EDWARD FITZGERALD TO HIS MOTHER.

St. John's, New Brunswick, July 8, 1788.

Here I am, after a very long and fatiguing
journey. I had no idea of what it was : it was

more like a campaign than any thing else, except in one material point—that of having no danger. I should have enjoyed it most completely but for the mosquitoes, but they took off a great deal of my pleasure ; the millions of them are dreadful : if it had not been for this inconvenience, my journey would have been delightful. The country is almost in a state of nature, as well as its inhabitants. There are four sorts of these—the Indians, the French, the old English settlers, and now the refugees, from the other parts of America : the last seem the most civilized. The old settlers are almost as wild as Indians, but lead a very comfortable life : they are all farmers, and live entirely within themselves. They supply all their own wants by their contrivances, so that they seldom buy any thing. They ought to be the happiest people in the world, but they do not seem to know it. They imagine themselves poor because they have no money, without considering they do not want it ; every thing is done by barter, and you will often find a farmer well supplied with every thing, and yet not having a shilling in money. Any man that will work is sure, in a few years, to have a comfortable

farm: the first eighteen months is the only
hard time, and that in most places is avoided,
particularly near the rivers, for in every one of
them a man will catch in a day enough to feed
him for the year. In the winter, with very little trouble, he supplies himself with meat by
killing moose-deer; and in summer with pig-
eons, of which the woods are full. These he
must subsist on till he has cleared ground
enough to raise a little grain, which a hard-
working man will do in the course of a few
months. By selling his moose-skins, by making sugar out of the maple-tree, and by a few
days' work for other people, for which he gets
great wages, he soon acquires enough to purchase a cow. This, then, sets him up, and he
is sure, in a few years, to have a comfortable
supply of every necessary of life. I came
through a whole tract of country peopled by
Irish, who came out not worth a shilling, and
have all now farms, worth (according to the
value of money in this country) from £1,000 to
£3,000. The equality of everybody, and their
manner of life, I like very much. There are
no gentlemen; everybody is on a footing, pro-
vided he works, and wants nothing; every man

is exactly what he makes himself by industry.
The more children a man has the better; the
father has no uneasiness about providing for
them, as this is done by the profit of their work.
By the time they are fit to settle, he can always
afford them two oxen, a cow, a gun, and an axe,
and, in a few years, if they work, they will thrive.
I came by a settlement along one of the rivers,
which was all the work of one pair; the old man
was seventy-two, the old lady seventy : they
had been there thirty years ; they came there
with one cow, three children, and one servant ;
there was not a being within sixty miles of
them. The first year they lived mostly on milk
and marsh leaves; the second year they con-
trived to purchase a bull, by the produce of
their moose-skins and fish : from this time they
got on very well ; and there are now five sons
and a daughter, all settled in different farms
along the river for the space of twenty miles,
and all living comfortably and at ease. The
old pair live alone in the little cabin they first
settled in, two miles from any of their children ; their little spot of ground is cultivated
by these children, and they are supplied with
so much butter, grain, meal, etc., from each

child, according to the share he got of the land,
so that the old folks have nothing to do but to
mind their house, which is a kind of inn they
keep, more for the sake of the company of the
few travellers there are, than for gain. I was
obliged to stay a day with the old people, on
account of the tides, which did not answer for
going up the river till next morning : it was,
I think, as odd and as pleasant a day (in its
way) as ever I passed. I wish I could describe
it to you, but I cannot ; you must help it out
with your own imagination. Conceive, dearest
mother, arriving about twelve o'clock in a hot
day at a little cabin upon the side of a rapid
river, the banks all covered with wood—not a
house in sight,—and there finding a little clean,
tidy woman, spinning, with an old man, of the
same appearance, weeding salad. We had come
for ten miles up the river, without seeing any
thing but woods. The old pair, on our arrival,
got as active as if only five-and-twenty, the gentleman getting wood and water, the lady frying
eggs and bacon, both talking a great deal, telling their story, as I mentioned before, how they
had been there thirty years, and how their children were settled, and, when either's back was

turned, remarking how old the other had grown ;
at the same time, all kindness, all cheerfulness,
and love to each other. The contrast of all
this, which had passed during the day, with the
quietness of the evening, when the spirits of the
old people had a little subsided, and began to
wear off with the day, and with the fatigue of
their little work, sitting quietly at their door,
on the same spot they had lived in thirty years
together; the contented thoughtfulness of their
countenances, which was increased by their age
and the solitary life they had led, the wild quietness of the place—not a living creature or
habitation to be seen,—and me, Tony, and our
guide, sitting with them on one log ; the difference of the scene I had left,—the immense
way I had to get from this corner of the world,
to see any thing I loved,—the difference of the
life I should lead from that of this old pair, perhaps, at their age, discontented, disappointed,
and miserable, wishing for power, etc. My
dearest mother, if it was not for you, I believe
I never should go home ; at least I thought so
at that moment. However, here I am with my
regiment, up at six in the morning, doing all
sorts of things, and liking it very much, deter-

mined to go home next spring, and live with you a great deal. I own I often think how happy I should be with G—— in some of the spots I see; and envied every young farmer I met, whom I saw sitting down with a young wife whom he was going to work to maintain. I believe these thoughts made my journey pleasanter than it otherwise would have been; but I don't give way to them here. Dearest mother, I sometimes hope it will end well; but shall not think any more of it till I hear from England. Tell Ogilvie I am obliged sometimes to say to myself, *Tu l' as voulu*, George Dandin, when I find things disagreeable, but, on the whole, I do not repent coming; he won't believe me, I know. He will be in a fine passion when he finds I should have been lieutenant-colonel for the regulated price, if I had stayed in the Sixtieth; however, as fate seems to destine me for a major, I am determined to remain and not purchase. Give my love to him; I wish I could give him some of the wood here for Kilrush.

MRS. RICHARD TRENCH TO MRS. TUITE.

LONDON, February, 1818.

We have taken a house in Gloucester Place. It has in my eyes but one fault, being too well

furnished, filled too much with that knick-knack-
ery I should banish were it mine, and dislike
guarding for another. Then I unfortunately
saw the lady who possesses it, or rather is possessed by it; and she gave me so many directions about covering it, dusting some chairs under the covers, and scarcely sitting upon others,
and watching over the extremities of the un-
robed ladies who held the lights, and not suffering the housemaid to touch their projections,
and not using leather to the gilding, not aught
save the breezes from the feather-brush, that I
was really quite sick of *internal decoration*, which,
like many other species of wealth, is often a
plague to the possessor. . . .

LADY SYDNEY OWENSON MORGAN TO HER SISTER.

PARIS, March 31, 1819.

. . . In a freemason's lodge the other night,
I was introduced to the Persian ambassador,
and had a good deal of conversation with him.
I am going to pay him a morning visit in form
to-morrow. The patriarch of Jerusalem was
also present. Their dresses, beards, etc., etc.,
were curious among the shaven Frenchmen and
women. Since my reception as a Freemason,
almost all the lodges have invited us around,

and given us most splendid entertainments.
Saturday last I went to one without Morgan
(who was engaged in his own lodge getting a
fifth degree), accompanied by Mrs. Solly, whom
I have made a mason also. We were left in an
ante-room whilst the lodge was informed of our
arrival, and were seated over the fire alone, and
gossiping, when, to my utter confusion, a depu-
tation was sent to receive me, in grand costume,
and an oration, which lasted twenty minutes,
was pronounced by a master mason. Of course
they expected a flourishing answer; instead of
which I was seized with one of my unhappy
laughing fits, not a little increased by Mrs.
Solly's face of wonder and awe. I was then
told I was to be received with acclamation, and
three rounds of applause; and with this comfortable assurance, I was led into the masonic
hall, amidst two hundred persons, who all rose
to receive me, crying out, " Honneur! honneur!" . . .

MRS. THOMAS CARLYLE TO HER HUSBAND.

SEAFORTH, August 5, 1845.

. . . Geraldine (Jewsbury) came yesterday
afternoon, looking even better than when in
London, and not *triste*, as R—— expected, by

any means. She has brought a good stock of cigaritos with her, which is rather a pity, as I had just begun to forget there was such a weed as tobacco in the civilized world. She is very amusing and good-humored, does all the " wits " of the party : and Mrs. Paulet and I look to the Pure Reason and Practical Endeavor. I fancy you would find our talk amusing if you could assist at it in a cloak of darkness, for one of the penalties of being " the wisest man and profoundest thinker of the age " is the royal one of never hearing the plain, " unornamented " truth spoken ; every one striving to be wise and profound *invitâ naturâ* in the presence of such a one, and making himself as much as possible into his likeness. And this is the reason that Arthur Helps and so many others talk very nicely to me, and bore you to distraction. With me they are not afraid to stand on the little " broad basis " of their own individuality, such as it is. With you they are always balancing themselves like Taglioni, on the point of their moral or intellectual great toe. . . .

CHARLES LAMB TO GEORGE DYER.

December 20, 1830.

. . . Poor Enfield, that has been so peaceable hitherto, that has caught no inflammatory fever, the tokens are upon her! and a great fire was blazing last night in the barns and hay-stacks of a farmer about a half a mile from us. Where will these things end? There is no doubt of its being the work of some ill-disposed rustic; but how is he to be discovered? They go to work in the dark with strange chemical preparations unknown to our forefathers. There is not even a dark lantern to have a chance of detecting these Guy Fauxes. We are past the iron age, and are got into the fiery age, un-dream'd of by Ovid. You are lucky in Clifford's Inn where, I think, you have few ricks or stacks worth the burning. Pray keep as little corn by you as you can, for fear of the worst.

It was never good times in England since the poor began to speculate upon their condition. Formerly they jogged on with as little reflection as horses; the whistling ploughman went cheek by jowl with his brother that neighed. Now the biped carries a box of phosphorus in his leather breeches; and in the dead of night the half-illuminated beast steals his magic potion into a cleft in a barn, and half a country is grinning with new fires. Farmer Graystock said something to the touchy rustic that he did not relish, and he writes his distaste in flames. What a power to intoxicate his crude brains, just muddlingly awake, to perceive that something is wrong in the social system! —what a hellish faculty above gunpowder!

Now the rich and poor are fairly pitted, we shall see who can hang or burn fastest. It is not always revenge that stimulates these kindlings. There is a love of exerting mischief. Think of a disrespected clod that was trod into earth, that was nothing, on a sudden by damned arts refined into an exterminating angel, devouring the fruits of the earth and their growers in a mass of fire! What a new existence!—what a temptation above Lucifer's! Would clod be any thing but a clod, if he could resist it? Why, here was a spectacle last night for a whole country!—a bonfire visible to London, alarming her guilty towers, and shaking the Monument with an ague fit—all done by a little vial of phosphor in a Clown's fob! How he must grin, and shake his empty noddle in clouds, the Vulcanian Epicure! Can we ring the bells backward? Can we unlearn the arts that pretend to civilize, and then burn the world? There is a march of Science; but who shall beat the drums for its retreat? Who shall persuade the boor that phosphor will not ignite? . . .

<hr />

WILLIAM COWPER TO WILLIAM HAYLEY.

WESTON, February 24, 1793.

. . . O you rogue! what would you give to have such a dream about Milton as I had about a week since? I dreamed that being in a house in the city, and with much company, looking towards the lower end of the room from the upper end of it, I descried a figure which I immediately knew to be Milton's. He was very gravely but very neatly attired in the fashion of his day, and had a countenance which filled me with those feelings that an affectionate child has for a beloved father, such, for instance, as Tom has for you. My first thought was wonder where he could have been concealed so many years; my second, a transport of joy to find him still alive; my third, another transport to find myself in his company; and my fourth, a resolution to accost him. I did so, and he received me with a complacence in which I saw equal sweetness and dignity. I spoke of his "Paradise Lost," as every man must who is worthy to speak of it at all, and

told him a long story of the manner in which it
affected me when I first discovered it, being at
that time a schoolboy.   He answered me by a
smile and a gentle inclination of his head.   He
then grasped my hand affectionately, and with
a smile that charmed me said : " Well, you for
your part will do well also."   At last recollecting
his great age (for I understood him to be two
hundred years old), I feared that I might
fatigue him by much talking, I took my leave,
and he took his, with an air of the most perfect
good-breeding.   His person, his features, his
manner, were all so perfectly characteristic that
I am persuaded an apparition of him could not
represent him more completely. . . .

BERNARD BARTON TO MRS. SHAWE.

WOODBRIDGE, March 2, 1837.

I owe thee a long letter in return for a very
long and delightful one, on the subject of lectures for mechanics' institutes ; and after a
month's silence I sit down to pay thee in what
Elia would have called bad coin, alias a letteret,
but the fact is I have been, exclusive of my ordinary desk-work, rather extraordinarily engaged since the receipt of thine.

I have, or had, two aged uncles, male aunts
Lamb used to call 'em ; not uncles of mine
exactly, but of Lucy's mother. Just after the
receipt of thy last, I had an intimation that
one of them, who lives at Leiston Abbey, had
been alarmingly ill, and the next Sunday I
posted down to see him. The day I spent with
him his younger brother, of seventy-five, died.
As he was my old master, to whom I served a
seven years' apprenticeship, I went the following Sabbath into Essex, well nigh forty miles,
to his funeral ; that is, I went on the day before
and returned the day after ; and the next Sabbath I went again to his surviving brother, of
seventy-nine, to tell him all about who was
present at a ceremony which his bodily infirmities had prevented him from attending.

Now when it is taken into account that year
in and year out I rarely go farther from home
than Kesgrave one way, and Wickham the
other, this unwonted change of locality has
put my personal identity in some jeopardy.
And never did I feel more inclined to call in
question that same, than in paying the last mark
of respect to my old master. The town, a little
quiet country one, about thirteen miles side-

ways of Colchester, was one in which during eight years I saw little or no change. Thirty-one years after I walked there as in a dream; the names over all the shop-doors were changed, the people were not the same, the houses, or most of them, were altered. It was only the aspect of the country round, and the position of the main street which I seemed to recognize as the same. The old market-place, a piece of rude and simple architecture, which looked as if it might have grown there in the reign of Elizabeth, and stood just opposite to our shop-door, was pulled down, and its place supplied by a pyramidal obelisk, bearing three gas-lamps,—gas! a thing the good folks there, I will answer for it, had scarce heard of thirty years ago. Out on such new-fangled innovations! Had I been apprenticed in London I should have thought nothing of it; but in a little obscure place like Halstead, a spot where all seemed changeless during my eight years' sojourn, I was fairly posed. Bear in mind that I was there from fourteen to twenty-two,— knew, and was known by, everybody, and was as familiar with all around me as with the features of my own face. Yet I stood as a

stranger in a strange place, with just enough
surviving marks of recognizance to perplex and
bewilder me. From fourteen to twenty-two
is the very era of castle-building, and mine
were dissolved in air by my return to the site
of their erection. No wonder that it has taken
me all the time since my return to become myself again, and that I have felt unequal to any
letterizing.

CHARLES LAMB TO BERNARD BARTON.

August 10, 1827.

. . . You have well described your old-fashioned, grand paternal hall. Is it not odd that
every one's earliest recollections are of some
such place? I had my Blakesware [Blakes-
moor in the "London"]. Nothing fills a
child's mind like a large old mansion; better
if un—or partially—occupied; peopled with
the spirits of deceased members of the county,
and justices of the quorum. Would I were
buried in the peopled solitudes of one, with
my feelings at seven years old! Those marble
busts of the emperors, they seemed as if they
were to stand for ever, as they had stood from
the living days of Rome, in that old marble
hall, and I, too, partake of their permanency.

Eternity was, while I thought not of Time. But he thought of me, and they are toppled down, and corn covers the spot of the noble old dwelling and its princely gardens. I feel like a grasshopper that, chirping about the grounds, escaped the scythe only by my little-ness. Even now he is whetting one of his smallest razors to clean wipe me out, perhaps. Well!

————

MRS. RICHARD TRENCH TO MRS. MARY LEAD-
BEATER.

BURSLEDON LODGE, July 30, 1811.

. . . The opening of your book on old age, reminds me of an anecdote of the late Duke of Queensberry, which I had from an ear-witness. Leaning over the balcony of his beautiful villa near Richmond, where every pleasure was col-lected which wealth could purchase or luxury devise, he followed with his eyes the majestic Thames, winding through groves and buildings of various loveliness, and exclaimed: "Oh, that wearisome river, will it never cease run-ning, running, and I so tired of it!" To me this anecdote conveys a strong moral lesson. connected with the well-known character of the speaker, a professed voluptuary, who passed his youth in pursuit of selfish pleasures, and his age in vain attempts to elude the relentless grasp of *ennui.* . . .

MRS. RICHARD TRENCH TO MRS. HAYGARTH.

ELM LODGE, March 21, 1822.

We could not let Mr. Brigstock have this lovely spot. If you saw the Hamble, as I do every morning from my bedroom, sometimes at low tide, " in windings bright and mazy as the snake," and at high tide in one broad sheet of dazzling splendor, which, when I suddenly open my window, reminds me of a ray of the Divine presence, you would see the immense difficulty to my weak mind of parting with any thing so beautiful. Mr. T. is firmer, but I think he *feels* as much reluctance. The spring has advanced with unspeakable sweetness and brilliancy. I am covering this place,—perhaps for Mr. Brigstock of the untunable name,— with roses, honeysuckles, violets, and early flowers. There are already a great abundance, all my own planting, but I am spreading them in every direction.

END OF VOL. III.

INDEX.

Freemason, Lady Morgan as a, iii. **272**
French traits, ii. **152–180**
FRIENDSHIP :
  Views of, i. **246–256**
  Deeds of, i. **257–264**
  Professions of, i. **265–277**
  The friendship of Cowper and Lady Hesketh, i. **279–291**
  Retrospections, i. **293–298**
  Elegies, i. **300**

Gainsborough, T., i. **136**
Gambling, ii. **37, 163**
Garrick, David, i. 83, 86, **118, 174**, iii. **254, 256** ; *to T. A. Arne*, iii. **265** ; *to W. Powell*, iii. **251**.
Genlis, Madame de, i. **102**
Genoa, ii. **184**
George II., ii. **10, 11, 51, 65**
George III., ii. **53, 54, 58, 68**
George IV., Hunt upon, i. **36** ; Thackeray upon, i. **37** *note*
German traits, ii. **147, 151**
Gibbon, E., *to G. Deyverdun*, i. **267** ; *to J. B. Holroyd*, ii. **186** ; *to Lady Sheffield*, i. **269**
GLIMPSES OF MEN AND WOMEN, i. **68**
  Allen, John, i. **186**
  Buller, Lady, i. **97, 98**
  Bunsen, Baron, i. **130**
  Burke, Edmund, i. **178**
  Carlyle, Thomas, i. **121–124**
  Chalmers, Thomas, i. **108**
  Coleridge, S. T., i. **137–142**
  Cooke, G. F., i. **91**
  Curran, J. P., i. **68**
  De Quincey, T., i. **172**
  Dickens, C., i. **187, 189**
  D'Orsay, Count, i. **101**
  Edgeworth, Miss, i. **116**
  Forster, John, i. **189**
  Gainsborough, T., i. **136**
  Garrick, D., i. 83, 86, **118, 174**
  Genlis, Madame de, i. **102**

    Vol. III.

Thirlwall, Bishop, *to* ——, i. 252, iii. 201 ; *to his sister-in-law*, ii. 145
Thrale, Mrs., *see* Piozzi, Mrs.
TOWN, iii. 1. (*See also Table of Contents, Vol. III.*)
Trench, Mrs. R., *to Mrs. Heygrath*, iii. 283 ; *to her husband*, ii. 24, 25, 90 ; *to Mrs. Leadbeater*, i. 96, iii. 282 ; *to W. Lefanu*, i. 92 ; *to her son*, ii. 91, iii. 16, 263 ; *to Mrs. Tuite*, iii. 271 ; *to* ——, i. 200
Turkish traits, ii. 236–240

University life, ii. 94, 96, 97

Valchiusa, ii. 193, 198
Vauxhall, an evening at, ii. 33
Venice, ii. 204–210
Victoria, ii. 64
"Vulcanian epicure," iii. 276

Wales, iii. 51, 54, 81
Walpole, H. *to J. Chute*, ii. 155, 157 ; *to Gen. H. S. Conway*, ii. 105 ; *to Sir Horace Mann*, ii. 20, 29, 37, 38. 40, 57, 152 ; *to G. Montague*, i. 294, ii. 33, 87
"Waverley," Scott's account of, i. 61
Weddings, ii. 1, 2
Webster, Daniel, i. 71, 72
WHIM AND FANCY, iii. 187. (*See also Table of Contents, Vol. III.*)
Wilberforce, W., i. 76, 77
Wilkie, Sir D., *to Sir P. Laurie*, ii. 238 ; *to Miss Wilkie*, iii. 121 ; *to T Wilkie*, ii. 138
William IV., ii. 61, 63
Wilson, John, i. 107, ii. 142
Wordsworth, W., i. 133, 135, 138 ; autobiographic, i. 19, 21 ; *to Sir George Beaumont*, i. 19 ; *to Lady Beaumont*, i. 21

Yanina, ii. 248
York, Duke of, ii. 66